D0989675

ARISTOTLE
Dean of Early Science

IMMORTALS OF SCIENCE

ARISTOTLE

Dean of Early Science

by GLANVILLE DOWNEY

Franklin Watts, Inc.
575 *Lexington Avenue, New York* 22

PROPERTY OF:
FRANKFORT-SCHUYLER CENTRAL
HIGH SCHOOL LIBRARY
FRANKFORT, NEW YORK 13340

NORTHSIDE MIDDLE SCHOOL

WD

S 3253

SEVENTH PRINTING

SBN 531-00853-3

Library of Congress Catalog Card Number: 62-13955
Copyright © 1962 by Franklin Watts, Inc.
Printed in the United States of America

Designed by Bernard Klein

To Shirley and Elsa Weber

Contents

ARISTOTLE
Dean of Early Science

PROLOGUE

The Search for Science

What is it made of? What is its purpose? What does it do?

These were the questions that the early Greek scientists asked themselves as they studied the physical components of the world around them.

In trying to discover what the world was made of, and how physical matter acted, they were indeed true pioneers. No one before them had tried to find rational answers to these questions.

The first Greeks had tried to explain the phenomena of nature by inventing gods—Zeus, the king of the gods, who hurled the thunder and lightning—Apollo who drove the fiery chariot of the sun—Poseidon, the god of earthquakes, and so on. But the philosophers sought something more acceptable—as they thought—to human reason. They had to start from the beginning, without any of the tools or instruments that later scientists had at their disposal. The Greeks had no microscopes—in fact they did not even have eyeglasses. There were no cameras, no Bunsen burners, none of the marvelous laboratory apparatus that is available today. However, the Greeks could divide the physical world into what they took to be its basic elements—earth, air, fire and water; and, for them, the question that faced the serious investigator was how these elements were combined to make up the world they found around them.

This investigation was carried on primarily by the powers of the human mind. Surely, the Greeks thought, the mind was a splendid tool—one of the most delicate, and potentially one of the most precise instruments that one could imagine. They discovered the uses of the mind for philosophical and scientific speculation, and they realized that it was astonishing what this mind could do—all by itself. Indeed, there seemed to be nothing that the human brain could not grasp and make its own.

This was the intellectual world into which Aristotle was born. It was a world of curiosity and investigation. By the time he died, he had revolutionized scientific thinking among the Greeks.

What was it, in the world of that day, that caused a man like Aristotle to do what he did? What impelled him? What prepared him for his work? What was it that made it possible for this work to be done?

How much of Aristotle's total accomplishments were original with himself, and how much grew out of the work of the earlier thinkers who were groping after what he found?

These questions, and the answers to them, can teach us much about ourselves, for our world of science goes straight back to Aristotle's accomplishment.

In modern terminology, what Aristotle achieved would be called a scientific "breakthrough." His story is one of the most fascinating chapters in the whole history of science and of human thought. He is one of that small group of men whom everyone, without any question, would name as one of the immortals of science.

Boyhood in Macedonia

It was in the year 384 B.C. that Aristotle, son of Nicomachus and Phaestis, was born in the little town of Stagira on the peninsula of Chalcidice in northern Greece —the peninsula that stretches out three promontories like fingers into the Aegean Sea. It was also the year in which the great Greek orator Demosthenes was born. The philosopher Socrates had been executed in Athens fifteen years before. The cities of Greece had been at war with one another and with Persia, but the war had been brought to an end two years previously. But, while Aristotle was still an infant, the "King's Peace" that ended the war was followed by new wars among the independent city-states of Greece. Meanwhile Athens, the great intellectual and artistic center of Greece, was still trying to expand its commerce and the other city-states were resisting.

The town in which Aristotle was born was a typical Greek community, speaking the same dialect that was spoken in the Grecian cities along the coast of Asia Minor. True, Athens had been influential politically and commercially in all of this part of Greece, but Athens' "Golden Age" had passed. She was still a wealthy and powerful city-state, but the Peloponnesian War, which had lasted twenty-seven years and ended just twenty years before Aristotle was born, had swept away her lands and power. What had been the vast Athenian Empire had now become a single city. Athenian culture still flourished, but the political power of Athens did not extend much farther than the city walls.

A new power was rising in this part of the world—the kingdom of Macedonia, which bordered Greece on the north. At the time of Aristotle's birth, Macedonia was still fairly small and loosely organized, but Aristotle would live to see this little kingdom become the mighty Macedonian Empire under the leadership of one of Aristotle's own students—Alexander the Great.

Stagira, although a part of Greece, was much closer to Macedonia than to Athens. Thus it was not strange that Macedonia should have a more direct influence on Aristotle's early years than Athens.

Aristotle's family were people of consequence in Stagira. His father was a physician of outstanding reputation. In fact, he became so well known and respected that he was invited to the Macedonian royal court, at the city of Pella, to become the personal physician of the king, Amyntas II. Thus it was that Aristotle passed some of his boyhood among the Macedonians.

The people of Macedonia were not exactly Greeks, although they spoke a language which was akin to Greek. However, the kings themselves claimed to be of pure Grecian stock, and they were eager to bring their country up to a par with the Greek city-states in wealth and power. These Macedonian kings were men of energy, ambition and ability, and Aristotle as a boy had a chance to see something of King Amyntas. The king had come to like his physician, Nicomachus, and the two became good friends. Moreover, the physician's son was a bright lad, and the king was interested in him.

Nicomachus belonged to the physicians' clan which was called the "sons of Asclepius," the god of healing. The medical profession was hereditary among the members of this clan, and it was natural to expect that Aristotle would follow his father's profession. Medicine in those days was far from being an exact science, and every physician had to depend to a great extent on his own resources. Instruction was largely personal, being passed on by a physician to the students who, like apprentices, gathered about him. There were no medical schools as such, and few textbooks. The treatment of disease was based on observation and on trial and error. Thus, each physician had to learn to work and to think for himself.

A descendant of physicians, and proud of his profession, Nicomachus hoped fervently that his son would follow in his career. As soon as it was possible, he began to guide the development of his son's mind. The boy's native intelligence responded. Nicomachus showed his son how man is the only living creature that can both think and speak intelligibly. True, some animals seem to think to some extent—dogs, for example, and horses to a lesser degree—but they cannot communicate in words what they are thinking. Since man can think, he wants to know. He wants to understand all that he sees about him.

Young Aristotle understood all this quite readily and, as he grew older, Nicomachus was able to teach him more and more how to observe the things he found around him —people, animals, plants, rocks, rivers and lakes and what lived in them, and the weather. Nicomachus explained to his son that an intelligent man must be able to learn what there is to be known about all of these things. If the boy was to be a physician and deal with man and his illnesses, he must have knowledge of many things—a knowledge both practical and theoretical. What Nicomachus could do, while his son was still young, was to show him what kinds of knowledge there were, and how to look for them.

Above all, it was the boy's powers of observation that needed to be trained; here Nicomachus' own interest, as well as the boy's natural talent, emerged. There were no "departments" of science in those days, and the scientist— or "philosopher," as he was called—had to be competent in all branches of scientific study. But Aristotle early showed a special aptitude for what would today be called biology; and it was this specialty, together with a general interest in the physical sciences, that marked all of his work throughout his life.

With only the simplest instruments then available, Nicomachus taught his son to dissect plants and animals, and showed him what to look for. The work was not easy because there were no preservatives, and it was difficult to keep specimens for any length of time. Nevertheless, Nicomachus, who himself had been trained by these methods, knew that the best thing he could do for his son was to train him to observe and compare, to analyze structure and function. Nicomachus realized that if his son mastered these techniques so thoroughly that they became instinctive to his thinking, he would have the best possible foundation for medical studies.

Then, as soon as his son was old enough, Nicomachus allowed the boy to act as his assistant when he was treating his patients. Here he was able to pass on to his son some of his own enthusiasm and dedication to his work.

At the same time, the boy was receiving the traditional Greek education; and, since Nicomachus enjoyed a comfortable income from his profession, he was able to send his son to the best available teachers. The boy read Homer, the dramatic poets, and Herodotus, the great traveler and historian. The study of Homer and the poets was the basis for moral training and the formation of character, for they showed humanity in all its aspects; in them, one could study the motives of human conduct and see the consequences of men's choices and actions. Greek lads of that day also learned the principles of correct writing and public speaking. Gymnastics, too, was an essential part of education, and the course of study included music and dancing, which were considered necessary for graceful deportment.

Aristotle was indeed fortunate in being able to enjoy the best education then available. There were no free public schools in ancient times, and parents had to pay whatever they could to have their children educated. Children whose families could not pay for schooling—laborers and slaves, for example—simply did not get an education. Thus, the rate of illiteracy was high, but this was taken for granted as a part of the normal order of things. Occasionally, a man of ample fortune would pay for the schooling of a poor boy, but this was the exception rather than the rule.

Then, too, family life was less secure than it was in later times. In those days, people were at the mercy of diseases which can now be cured, but for which there was then no known remedy. Pneumonia, appendicitis, tuberculosis, smallpox and many other such diseases were often fatal.

So it was not an unusual thing that, when Aristotle's parents both died of disease while he was still a boy, he became the ward of a relative named Proxenus.

Fortunately, Aristotle had inherited his father's estate, making it financially possible for him to continue his education. When he was eighteen and had gone as far as the local schools could take him, his guardian sent him to Athens.

T W O

Student Days in Athens

Young Aristotle was intensely curious to see
Athens. It was still the most famous city in Greece, in spite
of the damage brought on by the Peloponnesian War.
Commercial prosperity and a highly developed overseas
trade had brought the Athenians leisure and wealth. Thus,
the city had become not only one of the handsomest in the
Greek world, but also a center of learning and intellectual
life which attracted students and philosophers from every
part of Greece and its colonies. Socrates, the great teacher,
had been succeeded by his pupil, Plato, whose school,
called the Academy, was now in its twentieth year of activity. It was to the Academy that Aristotle was being sent.

As the ship on which Aristotle sailed drew near the
Peiraeus, the harbor of Athens, the passengers could first
make out the tall rock of the Acropolis. It was surmounted
by the gleaming marble Temple of the Goddess Athena,
patron deity of the city and the symbol of wisdom.

After he had landed, Aristotle made his way over the
four-mile road which led from the harbor to the city. Soon
he could see behind the city walls the white houses and
marble temples clustered around the foot of the Acropolis.
The sights of the famous city—its elevated aqueduct

bringing water across the plain from the mountains, the great agora or market place with its public buildings, the Acropolis with its temples, and the great theater on the south slope of the rock—all of these did not detain Aristotle long. There would be time for sightseeing later. What mattered was the Academy, and he made his way there at once.

Plato's establishment took its name from a public park located outside the walls to the north of the city, which according to some had been the property of a man named Academus. Others said that Academus had been a local hero, a semi-divine being, who had been worshiped there. At any rate, the Academy was now a grove of sacred trees, about a quarter of a mile in diameter. The grove had been enclosed by a wall and dedicated to Athena, although there were altars in honor of other gods and heroes as well. Shady paths had been laid out, and there were running tracks, bordered by colonnades, for athletes. This pleasant place had also become one of the favorite afternoon walks of the Athenians.

It was here, in this peaceful spot, that Plato had originally gathered his pupils for lectures and conversations. But Plato also owned some property north of the park, toward the hill of Colonus, and it was there that he was teaching when Aristotle came to join the school.

Plato was now about fifty years old, and at the height of his career. In the twenty years of its existence, the school had come to be a remarkable institution, boasting an ever-growing number of students and research scholars. It was like no other place of learning that Aristotle had ever seen, for it was at the same time a school, a center for advanced research, and a community of scholars, with the whole establishment dominated and directed by the greatest teacher in Greece at that time. Plato's philosophical dialogues, together with his treatise *The Republic,* a study of the ideal state, had carried on the work of his master Socrates. Indeed, Plato had created from that work a new method of study, and it was this that Aristotle had come to learn.

The company that Aristotle found at the Academy was quite diversified. There were boys in their late teens like himself, attending the lectures and discussions of the master; but there were also many men of forty and older who had been with Plato for years. These men had stayed on at the Academy to conduct their own research, which had grown out of their earlier studies with Plato.

The Academy was an institution devoted to every form of knowledge. Philosophy, mathematics, music, astronomy, physics, and biology were all studied because they represented the various branches of human knowledge. And every intelligent and cultivated man was expected to be familiar with all these subjects, for they were parts of the world of knowledge making up the whole.

Moreover, there were no degrees and there was no minimum course of study at the Academy. A student who had the ability and the financial resources might stay as long as he pleased, and pursue whatever lines of inquiry attracted him. It was at this point that some men began to be "specialists." However, they had all had the same fundamental training, and they were all working toward the ultimate goal that the establishment had set for itself—the acquisition of knowledge. For knowledge, Socrates had taught, was virtue; and so it was believed that study would make a man virtuous and happy.

Aristotle also began to realize how much of the value of the Academy depended on the conversations and discussions of the students outside of the classes. His new companions were of all kinds, and they came from all parts of the Greek world. The one thing they all had in common was a compelling curiosity and a tremendous urge for knowledge.

Aristotle sensed at once that here was a new world. For the eager boy from Macedonia, it was a wonderful thing to find himself in a community wholly dedicated to study and learning. It was equally wonderful to realize that he was perfectly free, with no obstacles or distractions, to learn all that the human mind had accomplished, and to try to discover what the true nature of man and the universe was.

At first, there was little doubt in the young man's mind what his career was to be. When he came to Athens, he had taken it for granted that he would become a physician, like his father. Thus he had thought of his schooling in Athens as an opportunity to acquire a broad scientific basis for his medical studies.

But after being with Plato and his companions in the Academy for a while, Aristotle changed his mind. He resolved that he would become a philosopher and scientist in the widest sense, not simply a physician. Knowledge was there to be sought; most of all there was, he felt, much new knowledge to be gained. Fortunately, Aristotle had the financial resources to remain at the school for an extended period; and, he was under no compulsion to earn his living, at least not immediately. As it turned out, he remained at the Academy for nineteen years, until Plato's death.

Probably no one realized it at the time, but in Aristotle

the Academy had received a student who was destined to mark out a new direction in scientific thought. The young man from Macedonia was at first only one student among many; but he soon made friends. One young man especially—Xenocrates—would long remain his companion and would be with him as his career began to mature.

From the start, Aristotle found Athens a pleasant place for a young man to live in. The warm, sunny Mediterranean climate was ideal for outdoor activities, and there were public gymnasiums where the Athenians gathered for conversation and athletic exercise. The young men of the city, including the younger students in the Academy, came together every afternoon for running and jumping, throwing the discus and the javelin, boxing and wrestling. Each gymnasium contained rooms where the athletes could undress before their sports, and a room where they could play ball in bad weather. Those who wished to practice boxing had rooms fitted with hanging punching bags of various sizes. Professional trainers gave instruction in the various games and sports.

Here in the bright Grecian sunshine, these open-air sports constituted one of the greatest pleasures of the student's day. Sports and games were taken seriously as a regular part of the educational program, for the Greeks had always believed that the body, just as much as the mind, must be carefully trained and developed. The saying of the Romans, "a sound mind in a sound body," was an echo of what the Greeks believed and practiced daily.

There was also much else to see and do. For example, there was dramas and comedies in the spacious open-air theater on the slope of the Acropolis. The plays themselves served as a means of education, since they dealt with human problems and human destiny. Here one could study man, and ponder the ancient Greek motto, "Know thyself," which was inscribed on the wall of the Temple of Apollo at Delphi.

Religious processions were one of the most delightful features of life in Athens. The most famous of the festivals was the Panathenaia, the annual celebration in honor of Athena, the goddess of the city. The procession to the goddess' temple on the Acropolis was formed of girls and young men, carrying the implements which would be used in the ceremonies, or leading the cattle which would be slain in honor of Athena. There were also chariots and cavalry. After the sacrifices, the meat of the slain animals was distributed among the people. This procession seemed to typify the prosperity of Athens together with the wealth that came to it from its flourishing overseas trade in pottery and olive oil.

This same prosperity could also be seen in the market place, where practically anything that one needed could be bought. Everything was sold together; one could find figs, grapes, turnips, pears, apples, roses, honeycombs, peas, lamps and water clocks—all set out beside each other on tables and stands. A passerby could at any time pause and watch a potter, or a furniture maker at work in his shop.

Yet the magnificent temples and public buildings were in striking contrast to the plainness of the city as a whole. Athens in its residential quarters was in fact rather shabby, with twisting narrow streets lined with mud brick houses, mostly of one story, designed around an interior courtyard open to the sky. Moreover, the houses of the rich and those of the poor stood side by side and, except in size, there was little else to distinguish them. To the Athenian, who spent most of his time in public and in the company of his friends, his house was chiefly meant as quarters for his family, and a place for himself to sleep.

As Aristotle himself joined in the public life of the city, he realized that what he was seeing was the Greek city in its most highly developed form. For a Greek believed that it was in his life as a citizen, as a member of a community, that man found his truest self-expression. Indeed, the Greek city was regarded as the place where people came together for the purposeful pursuit of a better life.

THREE

Greek Science Before Aristotle

W hat was the world?

The work of the Academy—indeed its very existence—represented the Greek belief that man was the center of the visible world. Therefore, the human mind ought to be able to solve any problem that man encountered as he studied the world around him. Man, being curious by nature, is also endowed with intelligence. Thus, it was inevitable that he should want to know the reasons for the things he saw in the world—including himself. Or, if one could not find the reasons why certain things in nature existed, one could at least determine what they were made of, and what caused them to function.

When the mythological and the magical explanations—so beautifully recorded by Homer and the other early poets—no longer satisfied the rational Greek mind, Greek thinkers set out to try to answer all these questions on the basis of human reason alone.

Young Aristotle, as he read and listened to the lectures at the Academy, perceived that earlier scientific thought had gone through two phases. Philosophers had first devoted themselves to investigation of the nature of the physical world and the nature of matter—that is, the nature of the substance or substances out of which the world and the visible objects of nature are formed. This subject had been explored by a whole series of investigators.

Then came a second phase in which philosophers turned to a study of man himself—his nature and his conduct. It was along these lines that Socrates and Plato had worked. The division of interest seemed only natural, they reasoned, because man already had some knowledge and understanding of himself and his fellows, and it might seem natural to begin the study with him. On the other hand, the silent objects of nature could not communicate with man and reveal their history to him.

Indeed, the initial questions of the early scientists were the very questions that men first ask while they are small children: What are the objects that we see? How are they made? Why do some things move while others do not?

To answer these questions, every thinker—every "philosopher"—felt free to set out on his own voyage of discovery. There were no instruments and equipment for technical investigations, no laboratories, no research libraries, no scientific periodicals, no congresses at which scientists might meet, exchange ideas, and learn of each other's work. A man who had the curiosity to embark on these questions had to work by himself, depending on the resources of his own brain. These were the resources of reason which Greek thinkers—Plato and Aristotle foremost among them—were to raise to such a splendid pitch.

These, then, were the terms on which the Greek investigator had set out on the independent and original human search for the truth.

As a student of the Academy, in which the powerful personality of Plato dominated, Aristotle had joined eagerly with the others in the study of ethics, that is, the whole science of conduct and social philosophy which formed the core of Plato's thought. But, in addition, Plato understood very well that mathematics and the natural sciences were also necessary for the complete picture of human knowledge and activity, and it was to these topics that Aristotle became drawn.

Moreover, those at the Academy were well aware of the scientific contributions that had come before them. Indeed, the names of the early scientists were well known to every student there. The earliest of the philosophers who might claim the title of natural scientist was Thales of Miletus, one of the Ionian Greek cities where civilization flourished at an early period. Thales had lived about two and a half centuries before Aristotle's time (about 624 to 548 B.C.). He was a mathematician and astronomer. Doubtless with the aid of the studies of the Babylonians, whose astronomical studies were famous, Thales had been able to predict the eclipse of the sun which took place in 585 B.C. This was a real achievement, for eclipses had been regarded as supernatural happenings, mysterious and terrifying portents.

By Aristotle's time, none of Thales' original writings had been preserved. Books, copied by hand, were scarce and there were few libraries in those days; it was easy for what few copies of a handwritten book there were to be lost or worn out. However, there were enough references to Thales' work by later writers to make it clear what some of his teachings were. Thales, observing that the basic materials of the world seemed to be earth, air, and water, concluded that water was the principle of all things—the basic substance. Everything came from water; and every-thing returned to water. The earth itself was a flat disk floating on water.

Aristotle, endeavoring to understand this teaching, con-cluded that Thales' water theory had come to him from the fact that the nourishment of all things is moist in character. Even so, it was not clear to Aristotle how Thales explained the process by which the universe arose out of water.

It was obvious that this was not a final solution, for it had hardly won universal acceptance. Yet Aristotle realized that its real significance lay in the fact that it was the first known attempt to find a natural and scientific principle of the universe; before, there had only been myth and magic.

Another significant feature of Thales' work was that it attempted to discover whether there was not a single basic substance or principle behind the outward changes that we see in the world. This, Aristotle knew, was the question that all Greek philosophers and scientists asked, and it was interesting to see an attempt to work it out as early as the time of Thales.

After that early effort, many others had followed. Anaxi-mander (about 611 to 547 B.C.), a pupil of Thales, and also a resident of Miletus, accepted the conclusion of his master that the basic principle of things is some basic material, but he could not follow him in the belief that it was water. Rather, Anaximander concluded that what was at the bottom of the visible world was an indefinite sort of sub-stance, formless and featureless, which in the beginning was not yet divided and differentiated to make distinct kinds of materials. This kind of formless substance, Anaxi-mander believed, extended to infinity. Yet it is not clear how Anaximander supposed that this type of matter came to form the world.

However, there was one aspect of Anaximander's thought that Aristotle found very striking. This was his theory of the origin of living creatures and their development by a process of evolution and adaptation to environment. Life, Anaximander believed, was first produced when the earth, originally fluid, began to dry out as this fluid evaporated. In the heat and moisture of this process, living creatures were produced. At first, Anaximander believed, there were simple organisms, which gradually evolved into higher and more complicated forms by adapting themselves to their environments.

Thus, man was supposed to have developed from a fish. As the earth dried progressively, the high parts became dry land; and the creatures that had lived in the water moved to the land and adapted themselves to life there. For example, the fins of fish evolved into legs for walking on land. This notion was a remarkable contribution indeed to have been made at such an early date.

The Milesian thinkers continued to take the lead in this kind of investigation. The next of these was Anaximenes who lived from about 588 to 524 B.C. To him, air was the "first principle," because air is constantly moving. Moreover, without breath, or air, life could not exist. As air is rarefied and made thinner, Anaximenes believed, it turned into fire; and as the fire rose it formed stars. Condensation of air then produced clouds; and then, at successive stages, water, then earth, then rocks.

Later investigators added other ideas. Another contribution that supplemented Anaximander's theory of evolution came from Xenophanes who was born about 576 B.C. He was the first to notice that shells and fossils of creatures of the sea can be found inland, embedded in rocks. These observations led him to believe that the earth had originally been below the sea and had risen above it. Xenophanes also believed that the earth would at some time sink back into the sea.

Another part of his study suggested an improvement over the work of his predecessors. This was his conclusion that the sun and stars were burning masses of vapor. Xenophanes was also quoted as having said that "We are all sprung from earth and water."

A different point of view came from a later thinker, Heracleitus (about 535 to 475 B.C.), of the city of Ephesus on the coast of Asia Minor. Heracleitus was closer to the time of Aristotle; in fact, his death occurred only about a century before Aristotle was born. Heracleitus had the habit of putting his ideas in difficult forms, and thus people called him "The Obscure." Socrates was quoted as having said that it required a strong swimmer to get through his writings.

Heracleitus put forward two leading ideas. The first was that the principle of being or existence was "flux," or constant motion—a continual succession of changes. The second idea followed out of this. Since fire is the most changeable of all the elements, all things are basically composed of fire, or developed out of fire.

Fire, to Heracleitus, was specifically connected with life and reason. It was the rational element in all things—the soul, for instance, was fire. Further, fire had the property of changing itself into air; air could transform itself into water, and water could turn itself into earth. Heracleitus' doctrine was not easy to develop, and one of his followers wrote that "the whole perceptible world is always in a state of flux, and it is not possible to have scientific knowledge of it."

Aristotle, as he studied all these theories, sought always to determine what the basic contribution was of each and what it was that their authors were really seeking. The very variety of these doctrines that had been put forward showed that there was not one of them that could positively be regarded as correct by everyone. But Aristotle saw that if he was to make his own contribution to human knowledge, he must know what his predecessors had sought to do.

Still another theory, and a well-known one, proposed by a man who had lived just a century before Aristotle, was the doctrine of Empedocles of Sicily (about 495 to 435 b.c.). This was the theory that there were four elements—earth, air, fire and water. These Empedocles thought to be the roots or bases of all things. Every other kind of matter or substance was explained as a mixture, in varying proportions, of these four elements. Further, the universally operating processes, which brought things into being or destroyed them, were the opposing forces of love and hate, or harmony and discord. Empedocles' thought marked an advance in that it was a genuine effort to distinguish different kinds of basic elements.

But, as an example of pure speculative reasoning, the thought of the "atomists," Leucippus and Democritus, was perhaps the most ingenious yet. Born about 460 b.c., these two men, supplementing one another's work, evolved a doctrine which was to have a great influence on the history of scientific thought. They believed that if one were able to subdivide matter, or physical substance, far enough, one must come eventually to units that were indivisible. These they called "atoms"—the word "atom" in Greek meaning "something that cannot be cut or divided." These particles, according to this early atomic theory, were the ultimate components of which every substance is formed. They are infinite in number, and so small that they cannot be seen.

In contrast to Empedocles' notion of the four elements, the Atomists believed that their atoms were made of only one kind of substance. Since the atoms varied not in substance but only in size and shape, the differences in visible objects were supposed to be due to the differing arrangements of the atoms of which they were composed. According to the Atomists, moreover, atoms are constantly in motion because they fall perpetually downward through space (there was not yet a theory of gravitation). Then, as they fall, they collide with each other and become entangled, thus forming combinations or aggregates of atoms; from these, formed in different ways, visible substances were assumed to be composed.

Earth, air, fire and water, Leucippus also taught, are conglomerations of certain specific atoms. Because these atoms are solid, the substances formed of them are unalterable; that is, they do not turn into other substances. Further, the process of the formation of the world from the atoms is the result of "necessity"; thus, there is no reason or intelligence in the government of the world. And therefore, all visible objects and all processes are the result of blind mechanical causes.

This bold doctrine, the most "scientific" and original of the teachings that had thus far been advanced, was taken up by the philosopher Anaxagoras, who was born in Asia Minor about 500 B.C. Anaxagoras settled in Athens, and was the first of the philosophers of natural science to establish himself there. A friend of the popular political leader Pericles and of the dramatic poet Euripides, he introduced a new idea into philosophy which later drew high praise from Aristotle.

Actually Anaxagoras started with the same basic beliefs as Empedocles and the Atomists. He believed that matter —the substance of things—was both uncreated and indestructible; every process of coming into being and of change could be explained by the mixing—or the unmixing —of the component parts. There were certain substances indivisible in nature, and that could not be derived from other things—for example, water, wood, bone, hair, earth and gold.

Anaxagoras' great contribution was the idea that the moving force behind nature, the cause of motion, change and all other processes, is an abstraction he called Mind. This was a non-physical force representing cosmic intelligence, an intelligence that rules the world. Mind, whatever it was, was the guiding principle in all nature.

Here was a doctrine wholly new in philosophy—one that was to give Plato and Aristotle their central ideas. Mind causes matter—in Anaxagoras' thought—to come together to form the world, and it controls the world after it has been formed. In this concept, for the first time, the material and the non-material, the visible and the invisible, were distinguished. That is, it was proposed that there is an invisible, intangible force which governs the whole *visible* world of nature; and, from then on, this distinction between the visible and the invisible was a basic principle of the work of the Greek philosophers.

There was, of course, much in the work of all these earlier scientists that Aristotle and his contemporaries could not accept. Yet Aristotle realized that these men had all made their contributions; if they had done nothing else, they had made clear to Aristotle what the problem of research was—and what was necessary in the way of method if the problem were to be properly studied.

It was an exciting time in Greece. Yet it was not only in scientific speculation that the Greek mind was expanding and finding new fields for exploration. Just before Aristotle's day there had been a great flowering of art and architecture in Athens, where the lovely temple of Athena, the Parthenon, rose on the Acropolis as a majestic symbol of the Greek love of beauty and order.

Indeed, the scientists who were endeavoring to learn the secrets of the universe were not the only Greeks who were marking out new paths. In the generation before Aristotle there had lived the famous physician, Hippocrates, of the island of Cos, who was the greatest figure in Greek medicine, and whose work with curative plants and herbs also constituted the beginning of scientific biology.

Hippocrates' pupils wrote down a considerable amount of their teacher's information on medicine, and here Aristotle could perceive the possibilities of further study of the world of plants and animals which his father had opened up to him when he was a boy.

New knowledge was emerging on every side. Aristotle would not have thought of it in that way, but he had come into the world at just the right time to take over from the earlier thinkers and build a new world of scientific thought.

The Greek Art of Thinking

Plato, the finest teacher in all Greece, possessor of one of the most subtle and penetrating minds the world has ever known, had dedicated himself to carrying on the work of his great master Socrates. Each of these two remarkable men considered that he had the special task of teaching young men to think clearly, and for themselves.

Yet in those days this was not an accomplishment that everyone liked to see young men acquiring; indeed, Socrates himself had been executed by order of the Athenian court because there were Athenian citizens who believed that the results of his work among the young men might be dangerous.

Fortunately, Plato had been able to escape public disapproval, and his chief aim at the Academy was the continuation of Socrates' work. Plato realized that, while the human mind was indeed curious to know, it was also lazy if left to itself. Likewise, it was easily dazzled by brilliant show and not always able, or indeed willing, to find out what there might be behind that show. The special gift that had been given to Socrates and Plato was the ability to awaken and train bright young minds in the art of speculation and thought.

The master of the Academy soon found out that Aristotle possessed an exceptional mind. It only needed the guidance and stimulus of Plato's talk and questions to set the young man off on his own independent line of thinking.

One of the things that Aristotle learned very early, as he listened to Plato and to the other students, is that there is a difference between knowledge and wisdom. May not a man possess a great deal of knowledge and still not be wise? It seemed to Aristotle, as he studied the work of the early Greek scientists, that it was vitally necessary for any investigator to be able to see where this difference lay—both in his own work and in the work of other men.

The difference between wisdom and knowledge, in fact, was the difference between trying to be a completely wise man, possessing the secrets of the universe, and trying to be a man with simply expert knowledge. True, one might seek knowledge for its own sake, for surely knowledge was worth having; indeed, this was what most of the people at the Academy were doing.

But to be a wise man without having exact knowledge— was that possible? Was that not perhaps the trouble with some of the earlier philosophers and scientists whose thought Aristotle and his companions were studying? Had these earlier scientists been able to achieve real knowledge? Aristotle began to wonder. Did they have the full and precise knowledge that was necessary for their theories? Could a theory be true if the knowledge back of it was not sound? Was it not for lack of exact information that so many of the earlier theories of the origin of the world were so obviously unsatisfactory?

These were the thoughts to which Aristotle returned

again and again as he listened to his friends, or walked along the banks of the Ilissus. So many men had tried to find the secret of what made up the universe—of how it came into being, and what the role of man was. Obviously there must be a true answer somewhere. And too many men had already claimed they had found it.

However, Aristotle reasoned, if their answers were not satisfactory, had it not been because they set about their work in the wrong way? Might not their methods have been faulty, or their reasoning, or perhaps both?

To Aristotle it was obvious that man wanted to understand nature. If he understood it, he could feel that he had mastered it. Indeed, man could not feel that he was free unless he could, in some sense, control nature by understanding it.

Aristotle became more and more convinced that man had thus far not been able to penetrate the secrets of nature because there had not yet been enough exact scientific observation and recording of facts. Only with such observation could there come method and orderliness.

Aristotle did not realize it at the time, but the demonstration of the universal need in science for meticulous observation was to be the foundation stone of his own chief contribution to scientific thought.

After he had been at the Academy long enough to have absorbed Plato's teaching and to have learned the master's ways of thought, a student was allowed to work by himself and to follow the lines of research along which his own personal gifts and inclination led him. Aristotle easily became one of the students who were permitted to do this. He enjoyed the privilege of keeping in touch with Plato, but at the same time he found increasing satisfaction in working out his own ideas.

Out of this new direction of Aristotle's thought there emerged several parallel developments. One was the establishment of the system of thinking according to rules of logic.

What is logic? It is simply the process of correct reasoning and the correct interpretation of facts. To be correct, such thought must be carried on according to accepted rules. Something like this, Aristotle saw, was essential for the foundation of any scientific work.

The system that Aristotle eventually worked out covered all the processes and the instruments of thinking—such as technical terms, and the properties or characteristics of objects. All of this study tended toward the understanding of right reasoning, as exemplified in what Aristotle called the *syllogism,* that is, a logical scheme of argument. Such an argument is composed of statements arranged in successive stages, for example:

> All birds have wings,
> All ostriches are birds;
> *Therefore*   All ostriches have wings.

Here, the first assertion represents the general rule, or *universal statement.* In this case, it concerns birds—all birds. The second assertion states a *particular case,* that is, in this case, a statement concerning ostriches. The third and final statement—the *conclusion*—represents the application of the general rule (about birds in general) in a particular case (ostriches). Thus it can be proved in clear and unassailable steps that what is true of birds is true of

PROPERTY OF
FRANKFORT-SCHUYLER CENTRAL
HIGH SCHOOL LIBRARY
FRANKFORT, NEW YORK 13340

ostriches. Such a conclusion cannot be attacked or over-thrown.

Similarly, a train of reasoning may go something like this:

> All men may make mistakes,
> All kings are men;
> *Therefore* All kings may make mistakes.

In this system of reasoning, the conclusion necessarily follows from the original statement. Moreover, it is easy for anyone to see that the *truth* of the conclusion depends upon the *truth* of the original statement.

Suppose, for example, someone says that all metals are solid, and that we wish to test the truth of this statement. However, we remember that mercury is a metal, and that it is not solid. Yet if we start by supposing that the statement "All metals are solid" is true, then we shall reason something like this:

> All metals are solid,
> Mercury is a metal;
> *Therefore* Mercury is solid.

This, as we know from our own knowledge of mercury, is untrue. But the truth can be proved by correct reasoning according to the rules of logic as laid down by Aristotle. Here we must start from what is *known to be true:*

> Mercury is not solid,
> Mercury is a metal;
> *Therefore* Some metals are not solid.

This is, very simply, the process of reasoning from something known or assured ("All birds have wings") to some-

thing else which follows from it ("All ostriches have wings"). If the rules are understood and followed, the student can avoid reaching a false conclusion ("All metal is solid"). This method of reasoning by syllogism was Aristotle's discovery, and he was very proud of it.

This same method of reasoning is also called *inference,* meaning the process of passing from a belief, to a judgment or conclusion. It is basic to all scientific thought. By inference, we recognize a statement as true ("All men may make mistakes"), and then we reach a conclusion which is implied in the original statement ("All kings may make mistakes").

As a result of this process of Aristotle's, a thinker was shown that if his thinking did not remain within the rules and meet the requirements, there must be something the matter with it. Moreover, using such a process, the student's mind could now be trained more carefully and fruitfully than had been possible in the past.

As a necessary part of the procedure, Aristotle pointed out that before one began a study or an inquiry, one had to understand the terms used—for the truth or falsehood of the argument would depend on the truth or falsehood of the terms employed. To avoid making errors, Aristotle, under the heading "terms," established classes or "categories" by which things could be described. All of these differed from one another, and were not to be confused with each other:

Term:	*Example:*
Substance	man
Quantity or size	six feet tall
Quality	white

Relation to something else	double (that is, one of a pair)
Place	in the street
Date or time	Monday, or last year
Posture or position	sits, or stands
Possession	wears clothes
Action	strikes
Passivity	is struck

These are the terms or descriptive attributes which must be used in the study and description of an object, in order to show what the characteristics of the object are. For example, we could describe "a man, six feet tall, white, alone, in the street, yesterday, standing, talking." The categories must not be confused; for example, "white" and "six feet tall" refer to entirely different things. Such a distinction may seem elementary today, but it was necessary when science was not yet sure just what knowledge was or what it meant.

The problem of relationship, too, had to be adequately described. For example, a man's hands may be described as double and, because they are double, they have a relationship with one another; for example, in being similar in size and shape. Again, being double, they are comparable to a man's feet, which have the same relationship of doubleness.

In this same manner, Aristotle established that there were other attributes or characteristics which had to be determined about an object before its nature could be fully understood. Some of these were called "classes of being," referring to whether or not an object existed and, if it did, how it existed. True, these are very abstract ideas, but they are important if we are to be sure of exactly where we are beginning the study of an object. These "classes" are:

Being—existing or living
Sameness—being the same as something else
Otherness—being different from something else
Rest
Motion

Other methods of description had to do with what could be called "common properties"—that is, pairs of attributes which could be compared or contrasted—for example when one compares two objects. These "properties" can be of all kinds, but there are certain groups into which they naturally fall:

Likeness and Unlikeness
Being and Not Being
Sameness and Difference
Odd and Even
Unity (oneness) and Number (more than one)

It was characteristic of Aristotle's purpose in working out his system of logic that he never thought of it as a division of formal philosophy—as it became in later times and is today. Aristotle did not in fact call his system "logic" at all. To him, it was simply "the art of analysis," a skill with its own rules—something akin to the art of literary composition.

This art of comparison and inference—that is, drawing conclusions—is called *analogy*. Actually, it is the way young children notice and learn things before they can walk or understand language. It is, as Aristotle perceived—and as we shall see later—the basis of scientific thought.

Perhaps most of all Aristotle was interested in the answers to these questions: What are the causes of our judgment of facts? What knowledge do we get by our senses—sight, hearing, touch, smell, taste? With what knowledge does our memory supply us, and what knowledge do we get by experience, that is, by seeing something, remembering something else, and then drawing a conclusion by comparing the two?

Aristotle was by no means the first Greek thinker to invent the art of scientific thinking. The early philosophers and scientists had speculated about the universe. Socrates and Plato had devoted their lives to teaching young men to think for themselves and to think correctly. Indeed, the great contribution of Plato's *Dialogues* was the fact that they recorded and demonstrated the Socratic method of reasoning and inquiry, further developed by Plato himself. Here was one of the foundations of modern science.

FIVE

How Are We to Look at Things?

What Aristotle was basically concerned with was an assessment of the point of view of Socrates and Plato in their inquiries into the nature of the world. To Aristotle it seemed necessary to transform the work of these men into a new method which—as he thought—would better explain the visible world.

In order to understand the task Aristotle set for himself, let us first examine some of Plato's basic ideas.

Plato's great achievement was to work out the theory of the existence of *ideal* forms of things. These, he taught, were invisible and abstract forms, existing in another world. The visible examples in this world—men, horses, houses, and so on—are patterned on these ideal forms. They resemble, and approach the ideal forms, but they never achieve the high state of development which is represented by the ideal.

Thus, as Plato saw it, there was an Ideal Man, an Ideal Bed, an Ideal Horse, an Ideal Tree, and so on. Each of these showed the best qualities, the purest and most complete form, of the creature or thing it represented.

The Ideal Bed, for example, had legs, a mattress, a certain size and proportion of measurement. A carpenter or furniture maker in this world may construct a bed, a painter may paint a picture of this bed when it is built; but the constructed bed and the picture of it will only be reflections or imitations of the Ideal Bed which serves as the original of all beds.

The meaning of "the ideal" can be seen even more clearly in the case of the Ideal Man. Human beings, it is generally recognized, have many faults, both in mind and in body. Each man has his own shortcomings and imperfections, depending on a number of factors. Each individual's faults differ more or less from the faults of every other individual.

To Plato, what this meant was that behind the varied imperfections of the human race we can see an Ideal Man, a perfect type of man, without faults, answering completely to all the requirements of a human being, able to carry out perfectly all the functions of a human being and to realize all the possibilities of the human race.

Thus, according to Plato's teaching, we must try to visualize the Ideal Man, the Ideal Horse, and so on, as the standard or norm with which we compare the men, horses, and other objects that we see around us. The ideal forms give the standards by which we explain to ourselves, and judge or criticize, what we see in this world.

Moreover, the ideal form is also a goal to be aimed at in any process of creation. For example, in building a house, educating a child, or carving a statue, we can—indeed should—have before us a vision of the ideal products. And, it is toward these ideals that we must strive.

In terms of knowledge and scientific investigation, Plato's system meant that the things that actually exist— men, horses, beds, houses, and so on—are to be explained and understood on the basis of the ideal concepts which possess the essential characteristics of these things.

Thus, in philosophy and science, when we study either man or some other part of nature, we are to study the object in terms of its ideal existence, its highest form. Actually, a follower of Plato's method may say that it is the world of ideal forms itself which has real existence, and that it is in this light that we are to look at the visible world around us.

This was, in fact, the point of view that Aristotle and all the other young men were taught when they came to the Academy. Under the influence of Plato's tremendous personality—his wisdom, gentleness, insight, the keenness of his reasoning, his wide knowledge—this must indeed have seemed to Aristotle and his contemporaries to be the true way of explaining the world.

But Aristotle was by no means a young man who would accept without question what was offered to him. More and more, as he pursued his studies and then began independent work, it seemed to him that Plato's point of view was not the best way to set about discovering the truth. True, as a system of idealism, as a way of conceiving human goals, it certainly offered high ideals. But was it the true way to scientific knowledge?

For Aristotle, the problem was: How are we to look at an object and how are we to know about it? Plato's method meant that we are to look at an object in the light of an abstract concept, that is, the ideal of the object. The horse we are looking at, for example, reminds us of the Ideal Horse. The particular horse in front of us may fall short of that ideal—it may be a very old, worn-out horse, partly blind, with some of its teeth missing. lame, even swaybacked. But behind this horse there is an Ideal Horse, an ideal representing everything that a horse should be. The unhappy horse we are looking at once had some of these ideal characteristics. But no matter how poor a specimen we may have come across, the Ideal Horse exists, and always will exist. Thus we think of all horses in terms of the Ideal Horse.

To Aristotle, this seemed wrong. The correct procedure, he thought, was to observe all the visible examples—all horses, for example—and then to base one's knowledge of horses on what one could actually see and study. One might, of course, arrive at something like an Ideal Horse, but the Ideal would be based on existing specimens, that is, on known facts. The process was, in a sense, a reverse of Plato's. Plato worked from the Ideal Horse to the actual horse. Aristotle wished to work from all actual horses to an Ideal Horse.

In other words, the question, as seen by Aristotle, was the relationship of the universal to the particular, or the connection between the individual and the total or mass.

What was actually involved, Aristotle thought, was the nature and the accuracy of our knowledge. How, indeed, do we know anything about men, or about horses, for example? In Aristotle's view, we can only have reliable and complete knowledge by *observation of concrete facts*. It is the visible, tangible object that is to be known and studied. If we are to make generalizations, and draw conclusions, it must be on the basis of observation and the collecting of information assembled from many observations.

Basically, Aristotle seemed to feel that it was impractical

to study something that existed only in the mind. If he were to follow Plato's example, and "dream up" an Ideal Horse, could he be sure that his Ideal Horse and the one in Plato's mind were the same? Far better, thought Aristotle, to study the things that are out in the world where everyone can see them.

This is what has been called the philosophy of *tangible things,* that is, things possessing substance and concrete existence. Plato and Aristotle simply had different ways of trying to visualize concrete objects. Aristotle's turn of mind expressed itself in terms of facts; his mind functioned in the objective method of thinking on the basis of things that are known to exist.

To minds which followed Aristotle's point of view, things are individual units and substances, each a separate individual. The universe is composed of a number of these individual things, making up the phenomena of nature and man. We can understand these phenomena, and know what causes them, only if we study the examples we can see and examine for ourselves.

Thus the knowledge of the scientist and the philosopher comes to him through his own senses and from what he himself can see and learn—rather than, as Plato concluded, from the development and study of the concept of an ideal.

While this seems obvious in a modern world where scientific ideas are formed, consciously or unconsciously, on Aristotle's teaching, we cannot really understand our modern scientific approach unless we recognize Aristotle's service in establishing his doctrine. What he constantly maintained was that only if a scientist has an accurate knowledge of particulars, of individual cases, can he go on and build up an accurate scientific theory of the universal.

It is out of a study of single examples that one constructs the general rule which governs the individual case.

For example, the scientist must know from observation and the collection of facts, that all metals are not solids. He cannot start from the abstract concept of the "ideal" metal—not being sure whether it is solid or not—and then proceed to generalize about metals.

Plato had indeed made a great contribution to human thought and knowledge by showing the wide possibilities of conjecture and speculation. The dreamer and his dreams are surely valuable. Much can come from dreams which may seem impractical at first, and then prove to be important.

Aristotle himself was developing a dream or vision of an organization of all human knowledge—which we shall examine later. In teaching the need to be authoritative, Aristotle was trying to fight against the danger, which was so common in his day, of inaccurate general statements.

This reaction against Plato's notion of Ideals led Aristotle off on paths of research that were quite different from those that most of the other students at the Academy, under Plato's direction, were following. Plato had taught his students to observe Nature in connection with the study of Ideal Nature, but Aristotle's new outlook on knowledge made it necessary for him to do more than merely observe —he had to take Nature into his own two hands and find out what it was all about.

It is generally thought that a good deal of Aristotle's twenty-year stay at the Academy was spent in formulating the methods of research that he would employ, then and later, in finding out the things that he eventually wrote down about the life-cycles, habits, and parts of animals and plants. Aristotle was probably more or less "on his own" in determining what research methods to use, since research had not been a part of Greek academic work up until Aristotle's time.

Of course, when we talk about "research methods" in connection with Aristotle, we are not using "research" in the modern sense. There were no laboratories, as we know them, and practically nothing in the way of scientific instruments. So Aristotle's method of research was still largely one of observation. But there are many ways to observe things. It is one thing to sit outdoors and watch a bug walk up and down a leaf on a plant. That was the sort of observing Plato and most of his students did. It is quite another thing to take both the bug and the leaf home, dissect them, and look inside to see what makes them the way they are. This type of "observation" was the method Aristotle used, and here lies the basic difference between Aristotle's way of obtaining knowledge and Plato's way.

We must not let the fact that Aristotle disagreed with Plato lead us to think that they were not friendly. They still had much in common, after all. Both had fine minds, and they certainly did not disagree in their love of knowledge. Aristotle's devotion to Plato is unquestioned; and it is certain that the wise and gentle Plato felt a strong affection for this brilliant young man, even if he did not always understand what Aristotle was trying to do.

A New Venture

To the members of the Academy, it must have seemed that their institution and its brilliant leader would go on forever. Having headed the society for forty years Plato, even in his old age, was probably viewed by the students as a permanent figure. Indeed, he had already been a famous teacher before many of them were born.

Thus, to the students, the end of an era seemed to arrive when Plato died peacefully at the age of about eighty in 347 B.C. He was buried at the Academy and all of the students joined in the funeral procession. Both students and teachers at the Academy were profoundly stirred. No one could replace Plato, and many of the members of the community wondered what they had best do.

Aristotle, among others, undoubtedly felt that the master's death marked a turning point in his own career. The time was in fact right for a change. Aristotle was now thirty-seven years old, still unmarried, devoted only to his studies. He had been at the Academy since he was eighteen.

Fortunately for mankind, Aristotle, with the financial resources of his father's estate, had been able to remain at the Academy for nearly twenty years of study and research. Now he could strike out on his own.

Whether Aristotle would have remained at the Academy if Plato had lived, no one today can tell. His later work shows that he was now ready for the independent creative career for which he had been preparing himself. On the other hand, Aristotle's attachment to his beloved master Plato had been so great that he would not have wished to leave the Academy while his revered teacher was still living.

In any case, it seems certain that Aristotle did not wish to stay at the Academy after Plato's death. The headship of the school passed to Plato's nephew, Speusippus. This man, a son of Plato's sister Potone, had been associated with the Academy all his life, and while he was less able intellectually than Plato, his taking over the direction of the institution had the effect of keeping the property in the family, for Plato had never married.

While it was obvious to everyone that Speusippus was less gifted than Aristotle, he was nevertheless older than Aristotle and it would have been impossible to pass over him in favor of a younger man. Some people said later that Aristotle left the Academy because he did not wish to remain there under an inferior head. There is no way of knowing whether this is true. Nor is there any way of knowing whether it is true that Speusippus had a bad temper and was attached to the pleasures of life, as Plato had not been. If this were true, it is not difficult to imagine why the serious-minded Aristotle left.

Whatever the circumstances of his leaving the Academy, it meant a major break for Aristotle to part from the companions among whom he had lived and worked happily for nearly twenty years. In those days, every educated Greek was taught to write poetry as a part of his general literary training. Aristotle set up a memorial, a marble altar in honor of Plato, and composed an inscription to be carved on the stone:

Coming to the famous plain of Athens
I piously set up an altar of holy Friendship
For the man who was so good that it is not right for
    bad men even to praise him.
He alone clearly showed
By his own life and by his teaching
That when a man becomes good he becomes happy.
Now that he is dead no one can ever do this again.

Nor was Aristotle the only person to leave the Academy. Evidently there were others who felt that Speusippus had inherited only Plato's office, not his spirit.

One such member of the community who thought that the time had come for him to leave was Xenocrates, one of the most prominent members of the group. A student of exceptional ability, he was loved by everyone for his quiet dignity and kindliness. His personality influenced everyone who came into contact with him. His specialty at the Academy was the study of moral questions and personal conduct. Later, although Xenocrates did leave the Academy for a time, it was not surprising that when Speusippus died in 339 B.C. he was chosen to be head of the Academy.

But at the time of Plato's death, Xenocrates and Aristotle, having long been friends, determined to go elsewhere together to continue their studies. Fortunately they had a prospect of finding an ideal spot for their work. This was the city of Assos on the coast of Asia Minor, not far from

Troy. Formerly under the domination of the Persian Empire, it had been given its freedom after the war between the Greeks and the Persians. Now it was under the rule of a remarkable man named Hermias.

Hermias had had a career such as few men, then or now, can boast. He had once been a slave. How he came by his freedom is no longer known. Slaves were sometimes set free by their masters on some occasion of family rejoicing, such as the marriage of a son or daughter. Sometimes they were set free by their masters' whims (Aristotle directed that several of his slaves should be set free after his death). Some masters allowed their slaves to earn money in their spare time to purchase their freedom. Hermias later showed such energy and ability that it is possible that he may have earned his freedom himself.

Once free, Hermias displayed remarkable qualities. He worked for a time as a money-changer in a bank—an exacting and responsible job in those days of the independent city-states. For, every city issued its own currency and a bank employee had to be able to recognize all the different coins and know their values, as well as knowing how to spot forgeries.

At any rate, Hermias was able to save enough money to go into politics—a promising career indeed for a man of ability. The Greeks, with their vigorous spirit of personal independence and their devotion to their native soil, still preferred wherever possible to live in independent cities; and a man who could offer them leadership and protection could make himself the supreme autocrat or dictator of a city.

So Hermias, beginning his political career as the leader of some villages around Mount Ida, near Troy, ended by becoming the autocratic ruler—practically the king in fact —of a considerable section of the coast of Asia Minor. He built up an efficient mercenary army and when he showed himself to be an able and vigorous administrator, some cities voluntarily placed themselves under his protection. His capital was the city of Atarneus, opposite the island of Lesbos.

It was after Hermias had achieved this high position that two members of Plato's Academy came into his life. These were Erastus and Coriscus, who had originally come from the town of Scepsis, which was in Hermias' territory. When they returned home they met Hermias, who had the good sense to ask their technical advice on drawing up the political constitution of the state he was establishing. The Academy among other things also studied the various forms of political organization, and its students were well prepared to advise a ruler on problems of administration.

The two philosophers from Athens were able to give Hermias such practical and effective advice that he decided they would be valuable to his regime. Accordingly, he organized an institute for them in the town of Assos, on the coast of Asia Minor, not far from the island of Lesbos. This gave the philosophers facilities for research and for teaching.

All this had happened before the death of Plato. So, when Aristotle and Xenocrates were considering what they might do, one possibility was to settle at Assos under the auspices of Hermias. They knew that Erastus and Coriscus were already there, and they knew the generosity Hermias had shown them.

Indeed, the king was delighted with the prospect of adding two such distinguished figures as Aristotle and

Xenocrates to his little circle of philosophers. In his having done so, the world is indebted to this ex-slave. Assos proved to be much more than simply a refuge or place where Aristotle might carry on his independent research. The institute in Assos offered him enlargement in two directions. It provided facilities for research in biology, especially marine biology, such as Aristotle had not enjoyed at Athens. Perhaps even more important was the opportunity to form a circle of students and to lecture.

This latter was an indispensable condition for Aristotle's intellectual growth, for it was by teaching that he found the stimulus for his own study and research; and, it was through his contact with his students that his own ideas were enlarged. His teachings were largely in the field of politics, and it is believed to have been here that he began thinking seriously about the book, *Politics,* which he was later to write. The institute at Assos had begun as a kind of outpost of Plato's Academy; but Aristotle's move to Assos meant in effect the foundation of Aristotle's own school. Moreover, this same school was to come to its maturity when he returned to Athens thirteen years later and founded the famous Lyceum.

The move to Assos also meant the beginning of a new life for Aristotle in more ways than one. He married the niece of Hermias, a girl named Pythias, whom the king had adopted as his own daughter. The couple soon had a daughter, whom they named for her mother.

Aristotle and his wife lived on the terms of closest affection. Pythias died before her husband did, and it was her last wish that they might eventually be buried together. Aristotle in his will gave directions that this should be carried out.

PROPERTY O
FRANKFORT-SCHUYLER CENTRAL
HIGH SCHOOL LIBRARY
FRANKFORT NEW YORK 13340

The fame of the school at Assos grew, and students came from Athens to work with Aristotle and to hear his lectures. Aristotle used the lectures as a means of working out and refining his ideas on various subjects. When he was satisfied that he had reached a proper presentation of his material, he turned the lectures into a book and then proceeded to work up new lectures.

One of the young men who came to join the circle was Theophrastus of Lesbos, son of a wealthy merchant on that island. He had begun his advanced studies at the Academy, and then was attracted to Assos by Aristotle's reputation—and also perhaps by the location of Assos, which was near his home.

A young man of exceptional ability, Theophrastus soon attracted Aristotle's particular attention. It was the beginning of a close relationship between teacher and pupil which was to last all the rest of Aristotle's life.

Life and work in Assos was pleasant. The city itself was one of the handsomest of all the Greek cities. Built on a hill rising from the sea, its houses were set on terraces with a splendid view over the gulf which stretched to the south. It also possessed a notable fortification wall.

The circle of students grew. But the political life of the Greek communities along the coast of Asia Minor was never secure. The Persian Empire controlled all of the inland part of Asia Minor, and for generations it had been the dream of the Persians to get permanent control of the prosperous Greek cities on the coast.

Hermias, like other independent rulers of the coastal cities, had been able to keep himself in power only as long as Persia did not make a special attack on him. It was thought that he was in touch with Philip, king of Mace-

donia, who hoped to extend his influence beyond the Greek mainland. Philip might have been ready to support the Greeks of the Asia Minor coast against Persia, in return for their allegiance to Macedonia. But this was all uncertain, and there were signs that the Persians were planning a new campaign to conquer the Greek cities. Aristotle and his friends began to feel uneasy. How long would it be safe for them to remain at Assos?

It was Theophrastus who offered a solution for the troubles of the school. His native island, Lesbos, could certainly be expected to hold out against the Persians. Moreover, Theophrastus' wealthy father and other friends could be counted on to provide new quarters for the community at Assos. The chief city of Lesbos, prosperous and beautiful Mytilene, would be an attractive center for the school and, as a seaport, it would furnish the same facilities for Aristotle's biological research that he had enjoyed at Assos.

Thus, Aristotle and his colleagues were easily persuaded to move. Indeed, the transfer was made just in time, for not much later Mentor, one of the most energetic and successful Persian generals, was appointed commander of the coast of Asia Minor, with orders to crush the independent Greek cities.

The little group in Mytilene kept close track of the fate of Hermias. He would have to be very resourceful indeed to defend himself against a general such as Mentor. The Persians besieged the king in Atarneus but were unable to take the city—the rather undisciplined Persian army not being accustomed to siege operations.

At length, however, Mentor accomplished by treachery what he was unable to effect by force. He induced Hermias to leave the city for a conference, then carried him off to the Persian capital of Susa. For a long time there was no news of him. Finally, the account of Hermias' noble death found its way back to Mytilene.

The Persians had been eager to learn what plans Hermias and King Philip of Macedonia had made. Hermias refused to betray Philip, and the Persians then began to torture him. Experts in torture, they were sure they could compel anyone to give up his secrets. But in spite of all the ingenious torments the Persians had devised, Hermias steadily refused to speak. He was tortured repeatedly, and when it became certain that he would not live much longer, the Persian sovereign allowed him to make one last request. In the midst of the torture Hermias answered, "Tell my friends and companions that I have done nothing unworthy of a philosopher." This message was carried to Aristotle. The Persians then proceeded to put Hermias to death by crucifixion, the dreadful method of execution which they had invented and which the Romans later borrowed from them.

Aristotle was deeply moved by his friend's death. He wrote an ode, or hymn, to Hermias' memory, in which he compared Hermias' bravery to that of the famous Greek hero Achilles.

The treachery and cruelty of the Persians only added to the hatred that Aristotle, like all the Greeks, had long felt toward them. Two years went by at Mytilene, and Aristotle's work expanded steadily. With his students, he was accumulating files of notes and reports which would one day, he hoped, provide the basis for the new sciences of biology and zoology.

Then a call came. Whether it was unexpected, or

whether it was something that Aristotle had anticipated, we do not now know. Aristotle was invited to be the tutor of the thirteen-year-old Prince Alexander, son of King Philip of Macedonia. This meant a return to the court at which Aristotle had spent part of his own boyhood when his father had been physician to King Amyntas. To Aristotle, this invitation meant a splendid opportunity to serve the Macedonian royal house to which all his sympathies were attached.

NORTHSIDE MIDDLE SCHOOL

Tutor to Alexander the Great

U nlike some dynasties, the royal house of
Macedonia had produced a whole series of able and energetic rulers. Each king, working steadily for the expansion of his territory and the security and prosperity of his
people, had sought opportunities everywhere to extend
Macedonian influence and to find support for his plans. In
the Greece of that day, composed of independent city-states
which were often rivals, such a task called for the utmost
diplomatic skill and foresight.

Philip II, who invited Aristotle to his court, was king
from 359 to 336 B.C. He had done much for his kingdom
both internally and externally. Indeed, it was a far more
stable and prosperous power than the Macedonia Aristotle
had left nearly twenty-five years ago as a youth of eighteen.

The cities of Macedonia, as Aristotle now saw them,
were richer and better governed. The kings had seen to it
that their people adopted Greek culture more and more.
Economic growth was favored by well-planned political
alliances with a number of the Greek city-states.

One of the greatest changes that Aristotle found was the
new professional army. In his own boyhood, Macedonia,
like most of the city-states in Greece, had only had a citizen

army. Men served when they were needed for warfare or guard duty, then returned to their regular occupations. It was the same with the officers—there were no full-time professional soldiers. Such an army was undoubtedly patriotic, and men were brave when they fought for their homes, but as amateur part-time soldiers they could hardly be expected to reach the highest level of training and discipline.

The intelligent Macedonian kings had seen the effect of such a military system on the complicated political life of Greece, and they determined that Macedonia should have a better army. Indeed, much of the rise of Macedonia was due to King Philip's development of a professional standing army of well-trained and well-equipped fighting men whose sole career was service in the army.

Furthermore, King Philip developed new military tactics unknown among the Greeks. He invented the *phalanx* formation, a solid mass of foot soldiers whose sheer mass and weight could either resist or crush any line of troops. He developed tactical wings to serve on the flanks of the phalanx for offense and defense, and trained an able staff of highly efficient officers. In addition, he studied the art of the siege of cities, in which no other army of the time had had much practical skill.

Such an army, Aristotle knew, was an effective instrument in King Philip's diplomatic undertakings. It proved its worth repeatedly in the limited wars the king fought with individual Greek cities. Moreover, the political expansion of Macedonia brought increased commerce and revenues by which the army was supported.

Thus the Macedonia that Aristotle found on his return was a rising power—a power on its way to becoming the greatest single nation in the vicinity of Greece. Aristotle also learned that the Athenian orator, Isocrates, had publicly called upon King Philip to unite with Greece and lead a crusade against the might of Persia.

For many Greeks, nothing more stirring could have been imagined. If the brilliant King Philip could accomplish this, it would mean not only that Greece would become a single nation, as it should be, but that the hated Persian Empire would be destroyed. Furthermore, if King Philip could not complete his plans in time, Prince Alexander might be the very person to lead the armies of Greece and Macedonia against the Persians.

Thus it was with a feeling of real excitement and keen anticipation that Aristotle took up his work in Pella, the capital of Macedonia. Nor was it only a source of personal satisfaction to Aristotle that the appointment had come to him. The king's choice of a tutor was a recognition of the importance of philosophical training in the education of a future monarch. Philosophers had long taught that a king must receive a special education, and that after he came to the throne he ought to consult philosophers for their advice on his political problems. There was the example of Plato, who had journeyed to Sicily as adviser to the ruler of that island.

So Aristotle was glad to see that a boy who might one day be one of the most powerful rulers in the world was to be entrusted to a philosopher for his education. He was filled with curiosity when he met the prince for the first time.

Young Alexander, then as later, was as handsome as a god. Strong and athletic, he had inherited from both his father and his mother, the Illyrian Princess Olympias, a restless energy and a passionate enthusiasm for life which were to mark all of his career. Even as a boy he exhibited the personal charm which later made him a great leader of men.

It would have been difficult to imagine a more fascinating pupil than Alexander; and Aristotle, who loved teaching and had himself studied under one of the greatest teachers of all time, found it a singularly challenging task to help shape this boy's mind.

King Philip was careful to provide a quiet place for his son's studies; accordingly, he set aside a garden, containing a temple of the Nymphs, outside of Pella at a place called Mieza. Here, in good weather, Aristotle and his pupil could have their lessons out of doors, walking along the shady paths of the garden, or sitting on the stone benches.

Together, Aristotle and Alexander studied the works of the great writers with which every educated person had to be familiar. They read poetry and discussed the thought of the writers on politics and personal ethics. Here, of course, Aristotle could be more than simply an educator. Himself an original thinker on these subjects, he was able to show Alexander not only what the philosophical thinker produced, but how his mind worked.

The boy proved to have a natural love for literature. The *Iliad* of Homer he looked upon as a masterly textbook of warfare. Later, on his campaign in Asia, he always slept with a copy of it under his pillow. This, moreover, was a special edition of the work prepared by Aristotle himself.

Aristotle also considered that a future commander of

troops should have some knowledge of medicine, and this proved to be a subject in which the youth was especially interested. As the son of a physician, and himself a pioneer in research on biology and zoology, Aristotle was able to make the art of medicine a fascinating subject. Indeed, Alexander became so interested in it that he later treated his friends when they were sick, and prescribed medicine and diet for them.

Aristotle also inspired Alexander with an interest in biology and natural research. Although Alexander probably did not do the type of painstaking research Aristotle did, we do know that he took a "scientific staff" along with his army when he marched off to his many conquests. The members of this staff would gather interesting plant and animal specimens and send them back to Aristotle in Greece.

From the beginning of their association, Alexander admired Aristotle and, as time went on, he grew to respect him more and more. The young man used to say that he loved Aristotle more than he did his own father, for while his father had given him life, Aristotle had taught him how to live a noble life.

The association continued for three years, until the requirements of King Philip's wide political activities made it necessary to place Alexander in a position of responsibility. When the young man was only sixteen he was officially named regent for his father, so that he might be in charge of affairs at the capital while Philip was away on his military campaigns.

This brought an end to Alexander's systematic education, and Aristotle now retired to his father's estate at

Stagira which he had inherited about five years earlier. King Philip had paid him a handsome stipend as royal tutor; with this, in addition to the income from his inherited property, Aristotle had no need to work for his living.

Theophrastus had gone with him to the royal court, and the tutorial duties had left some time for the research which Aristotle carried on incessantly.

Now, in Stagira, Aristotle found another opportunity, still with the help of Theophrastus, to press forward with his work. In his ancestral home he was able to spend five years of uninterrupted research and still keep in touch with the royal court at Pella, and with Philip and Alexander. But the political world was not as tranquil as the world of science, and after a few years there was a complete change in the situation in Macedonia.

King Philip, just as he was about to cross to Asia Minor with an expedition of Greeks and Macedonians to put an end to the power of Persia, was suddenly assassinated by one of his political enemies. He was only forty-six years old. His son became king at the age of twenty in 336 B.C.

Alexander, who had been acting as regent, was ready to step into his father's place at once and he declared that the Asian expedition would leave immediately. Aristotle realized that the task of conquering the vast Persian Empire must last for several years at least. With Philip dead and Alexander no longer in Pella, there was no reason for Aristotle to remain in Stagira. He had for some time wanted to return to Athens and organize a large school and research center there. It would not be possible to build up such an establishment in Stagira. His work was matur-

PROPERTY
FRANKFORT-SCHUYLER CENTRAL
HIGH SCHOOL LIBRARY
FRANKFORT, NEW YORK 13340

ing and reaching the point where he needed a group of students and researchers to help him.

Thus, in 335 B.C., the year in which Alexander and his troops crossed to the continent of Asia, Aristotle returned to Athens. He was now forty-nine years old, at the peak of his powers, and ready to begin what he looked upon as the most fruitful period of his career.

The Classification of the Sciences

Aristotle's ideas concerning the task of organizing knowledge of the universe were becoming increasingly clear. He wanted to be able to explain the whole universe—its structure and function—in a truly scientific way, on the basis of facts, carefully observed and correctly interpreted.

How was one to go about this?

Earlier scientists had tried to work largely on the basis of reason. This was a good thing—up to a certain point. But Aristotle was convinced that they had neglected to consider the physical facts adequately.

What did these facts show?

This was the question that Aristotle spent much of his life trying to answer. Out of his effort grew the modern concept of the natural sciences. Out of this, too, grew the modern concept of scientific method, with all its requirements of accuracy, systematic observation, and objective interpretation of results.

While these methods and concepts are taken for granted today, there was a time when they did not exist—when scientists worked alone, each man according to his own ideas.

It was Aristotle who changed this. The world of science

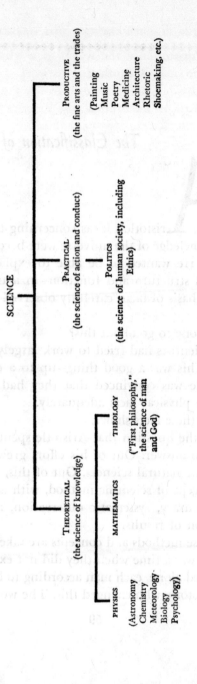

SCIENCE

THEORETICAL
(the science of knowledge)

PHYSICS
(Astronomy
Chemistry
Meteorology
Biology
Psychology).

MATHEMATICS

THEOLOGY
("First philosophy,"
the science of man
and God).

PRACTICAL
(the science of action and conduct)

POLITICS
(the science of human society, including
Ethics)

PRODUCTIVE
(the fine arts and the trades)

(Painting
Music
Poetry
Medicine
Architecture
Rhetoric
Shoemaking, etc.)

—and as a consequence the world as a whole—has never been the same since Aristotle did his work.

Aristotle divided the sciences into three general classes, which he called the Theoretical, the Practical, and the Productive (see the accompanying chart).

THE THEORETICAL SCIENCES

The Theoretical sciences aim simply at knowledge for its own sake. Under the theoretical disciplines Aristotle distinguished the following:

Physics

This category is different from the modern concept of physics. Aristotle's physics is a much larger subject than modern "physics." Since Aristotle's time, the subject of "physics" has undergone a great expansion. Research has progressed, new laboratory techniques have been invented, and practical applications of the results of research have multiplied. Physics today is a much more elaborate scientific discipline than it was in Aristotle's day. Aristotle used the word in the original sense of the Greek term *physika,* which meant "the science of natural objects," that is, objects or bodies which exist in nature.

In other words, Aristotle's physics deals with things that exist separately, and undergo change. They are "natural bodies" having within themselves a source of movement, or being by nature at rest.

Such bodies differ from the manufactured objects made by human art which do not have internal principles of motion and rest.

These "natural objects" include plants and their parts, and animals and their parts. They also include inorganic bodies and their elements, that is, bodies which do not have the power of change and motion within themselves, such as rocks.

In studying physics, the researcher in Aristotle's view is concerned with the observation of changing things, and with the conclusions that can be drawn from that observation.

Another characteristic of physics is that it is concerned with processes and properties which are native to the things themselves, and are not given to them by human action. For example, a horse has certain unique characteristics—as a horse—which are possessed by no other animal. But the characteristics of a wagon or a carriage are those which are given to it by the man who made it.

Another contribution of Aristotle's, so commonplace today that it is taken for granted, is the distinction between various scientific disciplines according to the subject matter involved. For example, Aristotle distinguished between biology and chemistry. This seems obvious to us, but the idea of making such a distinction did not exist before Aristotle.

Thus, within the inclusive classification of physics, Aristotle subdivided the following fields which today have become so specialized that they are scattered among separate "departments" in schools and universities:

> Biology, including Zoology
> Chemistry
> Astronomy
> Meteorology
> Psychology

We shall come back later to Aristotle's treatment of these subjects.

Mathematics

While physics in Aristotle's system deals with things that

  1. have separate existence, and
  2. are changeable,

mathematics deals with things that

  1. do not have separate existence, and
  2. are unchangeable.

That is, the subject matter of mathematics is numbers and figures in space, such as triangles and other geometric figures. These do not exist by themselves but are only used descriptively, to indicate the character of other objects.

Things such as lines, points, numbers, surface areas, volumes of contents, do occur of course in connection with the objects treated in physics. But the mathematician thinks of them as separate from physical bodies, and deals with them in the abstract.

It is in fact this ability to handle abstractions that makes mathematics possible. The physicist thinks of volume and quantity, for example:

$$
\begin{array}{r}
4 \text{ pounds} \\
-2 \text{ pounds} \\
\hline
2 \text{ pounds}
\end{array}
$$

To the mathematician, this is an affair of abstract numbers:

$$
\begin{array}{r}
4 \\
-2 \\
\hline
2
\end{array}
$$

Aristotle was much interested in the connection between physics and mathematics, and we shall return to this later after we have surveyed the rest of his system of the sciences.

Theology

Theology, which Aristotle himself called "First Philosophy," studies the subjects which:

1. we can know apart from body and motion, and
2. actually exist apart from body and motion.

Thus, theology, to Aristotle, dealt with:

1. the real principles of knowledge,
2. the real causes of existence and change,
3. the reasons why things in the universe are related to each other in a certain order.

Therefore, theology is, in the end, concerned with

4. God, as the supreme mover of all things in the universe.

Consequently, we see that it is the characteristics of a thing or an idea—change, motion, abstract existence—which determine whether it is to be considered as physics, mathematics or theology.

THE PRACTICAL SCIENCES

After the Theoretical sciences come what Aristotle called the Practical sciences, that is, those which have to do with human action and conduct.

According to Aristotle's conception of the world and the human race, the difference between the kinds of sciences depended upon their purpose. The aim of the Theoretical sciences is knowledge; that is, to Aristotle, man's interest in these sciences is purely in discovering the truth and acquiring knowledge. The truth which we discover in physics or biology is not dependent on our action or controlled by our will.

On the other hand, Aristotle's Practical sciences are concerned not merely with knowledge but with knowledge plus action. Action here is thought of as developing out of knowledge. This was the case with that branch of knowledge which Aristotle called politics. Again Aristotle's term is much wider than the modern meaning of the word. Politics today means the science and art of government, but this is far from being the sense of politics in Aristotle's system.

Politics to Aristotle dealt with men's lives—with their personal and public conduct and social organization; in fact, everything that pertained to public and private life. His book called *Politics* was written as a handbook for lawmakers.

A part of politics is "ethics," which is the science of the ideal human character and ideal human behavior. When Aristotle lectured and wrote on the subject of ethics, he was not only attempting to tell his students and readers what goodness is; he was trying to make them good.

THE PRODUCTIVE SCIENCES

While the Theoretical sciences are concerned with knowing and the Practical sciences with doing, the Productive sciences are occupied with making.

Today we make a very definite distinction between what we call "the fine arts," which are:

> Painting
> Sculpture
> Music

Poetry
Architecture,

and what we call the creative crafts or "mechanical" activities:

House painting
Carpentry
Shoemaking,
and so on.

The Greeks, including Aristotle, did not make this distinction. All the "productive" arts were on the same footing, and a "gentleman" was not supposed to be actively engaged in any of them. A "gentleman" must not make his living by working with his hands. The painter, the sculptor, and other artists occupied much lower social positions than they do today, and an architect was not very much different from what we should call a foreman or a contractor.

Even though the various branches of science—Theoretical, Practical, and Productive—can be separated by their subject matter and their purpose, they are still related. We can see this in the way that a mathematician and a carpenter measure a right angle. To the mathematician, a right angle is a part of a larger set of truths concerning lines, angles and surfaces, collected and classified in the science of geometry. To the carpenter, the right angle is the shape of a piece of wood which he finds he needs in building something.

So much for the classification of the sciences. What of their organization and their use?

The Organization of Knowledge

It is the business of wisdom to discover the causes of visible things."

This rather simple statement, put down by Aristotle in one of his books, sums up the program of his whole life.

Behind these words there lies a whole system of thought —the system we have just seen outlined in a chart. True, charts and outlines filled with the names of the great sciences are impressive. Probably Aristotle often drew up such outlines himself. But what, actually, did his classification of the sciences mean? What did Aristotle's work here signify in relation to our own day?

The scheme of the sciences grew, in the first place, out of the work of Aristotle's predecessors. They had set out to understand the universe, and thus they had created the scientific world into which Aristotle came.

One of the things Aristotle learned from the work of his predecessors was that they had not taken into account the differences between the kinds of problems they were studying. Chiefly, they wanted to know—yet they were not sure how to go about it. But their work showed, as Aristotle wrote in another of his books, that "all mankind have an instinctive desire for knowledge." Possessed by this desire, Aristotle determined to make a fresh start.

There must be a difference, Aristotle thought, between things which possess life, and inert matter: earth, rocks, minerals, water. This is the first of the differences that must be significant.

In the same way, there are obvious differences between men and all other living creatures.

But all these things—and here the earlier scientists and Aristotle agreed—form one universe, and it is the scientist's task to try to understand the whole of the universe.

As he came among scientists who had this vision and ideal, the special gift that was given to Aristotle was the ability to see that one must begin the long task by getting exact knowledge—so far as that was possible—of all the different parts of the world and the universe.

Thus it was Aristotle who first broke down the problem into what he thought its parts must be. Having studied the parts, one should then try to see how and why the parts fit together. In this way, one can come to have a better understanding of both the parts and the whole.

Knowledge, from this point of view, is one whole, just as the universe is one whole. The common effort of all science was to bring all this within the control of the human mind.

How was all this knowledge to be built up?

Here was another area in which Aristotle, seeing what his predecessors had accomplished, believed that much more must be done.

What was needed now was observation and recording of facts, which none of Aristotle's forerunners had undertaken. If theories were based simply on individual ideas and personal opinions, rather than on observed and recorded facts, the scientist might do harm rather than good.

This kind of thinking, in Aristotle's opinion, resulted only in vague and inaccurate generalizations. Socrates and Plato had worked all their lives to show people how to avoid these generalizations in thought and reasoning. Aristotle, trained in this tradition, saw that it was his task to show how such generalizations would be impossible for the scientist who devoted himself to the study of facts.

Aristotle had to develop his own techniques and had to find his material himself. When he wanted to dissect a wild animal or a rare fish, he had to find a hunter or fisherman who could locate and capture the specimen for him. In studying plants and trees, he had to discover where the rare ones grew, and he had to be able to obtain specimens of them at the proper seasons.

The fact that his former pupil, Alexander, cooperated eagerly and sent back rare examples of plants and animals which he encountered in his campaigns allowed Aristotle to study specimens he would never have found in Greece.

The work carried out over a long period of years meant the accumulation of a huge amount of notes and observations. To cite just one example, Aristotle collected detailed records of the habits, breeding, and bodily structure of some four hundred and fifty animals. These records alone would be an impressive amount of material for any scientist, ancient or modern.

In all his observations, Aristotle's principles were care and precision, plus common sense. He always took into account the work of his forerunners, but he also felt that the scientific investigator must pay attention to the commonsense observations of ordinary men. Hunters and fishermen, as well as farmers, had long and intimate acquaintance with the plants and animals with which they had to deal every day. Thus, whenever he could, Aristotle talked with these men about the things they had been familiar with all their lives.

Nor did Aristotle ever make it his habit to propose a theory as though it were completely new. When he came to lecture or write about any new subject or problem, he would first list past opinions and current beliefs, examine them critically, discard what was wrong, keep what was still useful, and then add his own contribution. As every true scientist does, he acknowledged his debt to his predecessors, and he was great enough to confess that he often used the work of other men.

Every scientist must develop his own tools. One problem that Aristotle had perhaps not anticipated when he began his independent work was the need for new technical terms. While the Greek language was a rich instrument, Aristotle was having to express ideas, classifications and methods that no worker before him had thought of. For these purposes, it proved necessary to make up words, or borrow words and adapt them to new meanings.

Some of Aristotle's new terms, which became established through his writings and are still in use today, are:

aorta	maxim
category	metaphysics
energy	motive
entomology	natural history
essence	physician
faculty	principle
form	quintessence
habit	syllogism

Moreover, help given by students was always an essential part of Aristotle's method of research. This help came in two ways.

As Plato had done, Aristotle trained his students' minds by having them discuss with him ideas that were emerging from his work. As Aristotle speculated about the meaning of the evidence he was collecting, he would confront the students with questions. What does this new piece of evidence signify? How does it fit with the other evidence we have already examined?

Aristotle had had the experience of every good scientist and teacher—discussion and debate in a group of serious students and researchers is bound to be fruitful both for the students and for the master. If the teacher, simply by reason of his greater experience, happens to know more about the subject, he can still learn something by seeing the effect of the idea on the student's mind.

This was one source of stimulation and scientific growth that Aristotle always depended on. The other was the actual assistance of his students in observing and recording material.

From Aristotle's lectures and books it is plain that students were regularly assigned to help in collecting the enormous amount of scientific information that Aristotle needed. They had to learn to observe animals and plants and to record their growth and their habits. They also had to learn to dissect plants, animals, birds and fish, and to report and evaluate what they found.

Only in this way was it possible for Aristotle to deal with all the subjects that it was necessary for him to cover. It was not always easy work for the students. There is one passage in Aristotle's book, *Parts of Animals,* that gives us an amusing glimpse of what went on:

> In studying living creatures we must omit nothing, whether it seems dignified or not. Even if we have to study creatures which are offensive to our senses, we must remember that they were made by Nature. Everything about them is important if we wish to understand the causes of things. In every form of life there is some beauty and something of Nature. In the works of Nature we can see plan, not chance. Therefore it is childish to think that the study of the lower forms of life is repulsive.

It is entertaining to speculate on what lay behind this last sentence. Had some elegant and well-bred young man balked at dissecting an earthworm or a frog? There must have been many creatures the students had to handle that were disagreeable both to look at and to smell.

It must be remembered that in the Greece of that day it was a well-established tradition that a "gentleman" never did any work with his hands (athletics and warfare were exceptions). Aristotle himself is described by his biographer as a rather small, delicately made man, accustomed to being very elegant in his clothing, his haircuts, and his rings. He was, after all, a member of a distinguished and well-to-do professional family, and he was accustomed to living at royal courts and associating with kings and princes on familiar terms.

Yet we may be sure that Aristotle never hesitated over a disagreeable laboratory specimen or a repulsive and odorous dissection, and we can picture him cutting up a fish or a chicken and explaining the organs to the students as he went along.

What was always in the forefront of Aristotle's mind—and in the mind of every scientist and researcher since his time—was that every fact is significant. Everything that can be observed—in biology, physics, and all the sciences—is meaningful and must be carefully studied. Every fact has some message for the scientist, no matter how unimportant it may seem, or how disagreeable to the human sensibilities.

Aristotle's desire to be able to organize the sciences and use them would, by itself, be enough to explain how it was that he came to construct his system of philosophy. But, in addition to this, there is another motive that can be detected in Aristotle's writings. This is actually the motivation that has always been present in the work of all scholars and scientists, whether they are aware of it or not.

Aristotle had written: "All mankind have an instinctive desire for knowledge." But Aristotle also realized that there is a special *pleasure,* unlike any other pleasure, in acquiring knowledge.

Once the urge to study enters a man's mind, it possesses an irresistible power. The philosopher and the scientist come to have a faith that knowledge has power to lift its possessor to a level he could not otherwise reach.

In the opening pages of his book on theology, called the *Metaphysics,* Aristotle studies this power which the pleasure of learning has over a man's mind.

Obviously Aristotle wrote from his own experience and from his intimate observation of his friends among the scientists and philosophers. To begin with he declared that there is a real pleasure connected with the three successive stages of learning—seeing, understanding, and knowing.

This pleasure exists in every man. A man may feel it in various ways, depending upon a large number of different factors—age, education, social and economic position, nationality. The pleasure is felt at different levels of consciousness, but it is always there.

Why does man feel this pleasure?

He may be enjoying himself because, by acquiring knowledge, he is helping to improve the material conditions of his own life and of the life of society in general. But this, Aristotle believed, is not the only reason why he feels pleasure in getting knowledge. That pleasure, Aristotle concluded, comes because man is realizing and fulfilling his own higher nature.

True pleasure, then, does not come because man is pursuing knowledge for selfish reasons—that is, for profit or for physical comfort. To the man whose circumstances in life make it possible, the highest pleasure is the acquisition of knowledge for its own sake. Here, Aristotle thought, man is coming into his own, true, higher nature. Indeed, this is the highest development of civilization.

Naturally, Aristotle realized that this ability to achieve knowledge and the pleasure of knowledge is not given to all men. The philosopher and the scientist have to be freed from the cares and distractions of the everyday world in order to do their work effectively. Aristotle himself was able to do what he did because he was never hampered by lack of money.

In order to understand Aristotle—and other scientists—we must realize the special enthusiasm that comes to the researcher from his work. It is a satisfaction like no other.

Thus, Aristotle himself could feel a pride and satisfaction in the fact that knowledge was advancing. Man could, he felt certain, look forward to the time when knowledge of everything in the universe would be complete.

The men of Aristotle's generation and the preceding generation—statesmen, artists, poets, historians, philosophers—felt that they had such creative power and that they were always making progress. They could look around them at the temples, theaters, and schools of Greece and be sure that they were advancing human knowledge. They were learning to master the world, and they felt that they were visibly making the world a better place.

So it was, Aristotle thought and wrote, that the scientist, in a society that was creative, took his own special pleasure in his own particular work. The scientist does not require the promise of material reward. If necessary he would be glad to do his work without compensation. Once the scientist or the scholar lays hold of his work, the work likewise lays hold of him, and thus it becomes his greatest enjoyment.

His writings make it plain that Aristotle was keenly aware of all this. Here, then, we see another side of his character which helps to explain his achievement. Partly growing out of his environment, partly originating within himself, his love for knowledge and his joy and excitement in research and discovery have been reproduced in all the scientists and philosophers who have followed him.

This will help us to understand what we shall see in the following chapters—the immense amount of patient work that went into the building up of Aristotle's new world of science.

◆◆◆

TEN

The Science of Life

The Greeks had always been very much alive
to the world of nature around them. They lived close to
the earth and the sea. They were accustomed to seeing
plants, animals, and fish every day.

Aristotle himself had always lived close to nature. His
father's early lessons had taught him to look with curiosity
and appreciation at every living creature he saw, and his
own natural inclination had responded to his father's
enthusiasm and skill.

So it was that, while Aristotle was a great all-around
scientist, he was at his best in biology, with its twin
branches of botany and zoology. Indeed, some modern
scientists have looked upon Aristotle as the greatest naturalist of all time.

Aristotle, however, was not the first serious observer of
nature among the Greeks. Long before his time, Greek
artists had been painting pictures of plants, animals, and
fish on pottery jars and vases, and on the walls of houses
and royal palaces. These painters were extremely skillful
and their pictures, which have been preserved, are extraor-
dinarily lively and accurate. Actually, the first Greeks

76

who might have claimed to be called "botanists" were the early physicians, and the men and women who gathered medicinal herbs and plants for them.

In those very early days of medicine, knowledge of drugs and diet was still very much an affair of trial and error. As the peasants and farmers doctored themselves and members of their families, a whole set of beliefs grew up in the curative powers of certain plants and herbs. There was also, to be sure, a considerable knowledge of poisonous plants.

Thus it was that in Aristotle's time, medicine and biology were in close alliance. In fact, apart from the farmers' and gardeners' practical knowledge of their plants, biology was almost an adjunct of medicine.

This connection first appeared in the work of Hippocrates (born in 460 B.C.), the most famous of all the ancient Greek physicians. Hippocrates and his pupils wrote a number of treatises on medicine, dealing with health and disease, diagnosis, diet, surgery, and drugs.

Here Aristotle could find both ideas and material. The Hippocratic writings were all based on firsthand observations, which the master and his pupils had actually seen and recorded. Aristotle realized that these medical records were very much like what he himself would have to compile.

Aristotle, it must be remembered, had no previous training for his task such as a modern student of science would have received. He had no reference books or encyclopedias. There were no experts whom he could consult. In fact he did not even own a book on natural history. Such a book did not yet exist. Indeed, it was his job to write one.

Aristotle's orderly mind saw that the first step was to

sort out and classify the different kinds of material objects and living things that one saw every day.

The first conclusion was easy. Nature was visibly divided into two kinds of objects and beings—those that possessed life and those that did not. Here are those categories:

1. Nonliving or inanimate nature: rocks, water, earth, metals, and so on.
2. Living or animate nature: plants and animals, including man.

Right at the beginning there were two differences between Aristotle's point of view and the point of view of most modern scientists.

First, Greek philosophers, such as Plato and Aristotle, felt very strongly that their field of interest and activity was the *whole* of knowledge. Their interests could extend to everything and anything. They were concerned both with abstract ideas and with concrete facts. Indeed, their investigations took in everything all along the scale, from man's intellectual life to the bodily structure of fish. The entire span of knowledge made up one whole and it was the business of the philosopher to investigate that whole.

In our own day, of course, science has become so complex that it is all that most men can do to master one special field. But such a program for an individual investigator was still possible in Aristotle's time, for in those early days of science, when the amount of the available information was still relatively limited, a man could be an expert in several fields of science at the same time.

Thus, Aristotle certainly would not have been satisfied

to limit his work to one field, even if he had realized, for example, that he was better as a biologist than as a mathematician or physicist.

The Greek point of view was responsible for still another characteristic difference between ancient and modern science. This difference involves the whole concept of what the aim of science is.

The modern scientist, ever since the Renaissance, or "Revival of Learning" in the 1500's and the 1600's, has felt that his first task and responsibility concerns concrete facts. The scientist first observes and records facts. He then verifies by further experiment the conclusions he draws from them. Finally, if it develops that he has made a discovery, he publishes his new results.

Obviously it is best for this process to be carried on in an impersonal and detached way. The more objective the scientist's aims and methods, the more confidence other scientists will have in his results.

True, Aristotle was the first scientific investigator to use objective, experimental methods on a large scale. But to him, and to other Greek thinkers, science—that is, science as they knew it—was not primarily an impersonal affair.

To Aristotle and his fellow philosophers, science was meant to be studied *in its relationship to man*. Man, to them, was the center of the universe, therefore one studied the universe, and nature, from the point of view of man and human life. Indeed, "know thyself" was the characteristic Greek motto inscribed on the wall of the Temple of Apollo at Delphi. Thus, to the Greeks, science was not an isolated activity to be pursued for its own sake.

This was why, when Aristotle began to study the organization of biology as the science of living nature, he included man among the animals. True, man was the highest of the animals and of all living things, but he was still one among the many divisions of biological classification.

Moreover, the world of living things was not something outside of man. Even if man was unique in the world of nature, Aristotle believed, he was still a part of the world. Therefore, he had to be treated in relationship to the world, and the world in relationship to him.

If things could be divided between the nonliving and the living, it was obviously more important to begin by studying the living part of the world.

In addition to man, there were two other great classes—plants and animals. Both, of course, had one important feature in common: they possessed the mysterious power called life. They came into existence, needed nourishment, grew, then eventually died and disappeared.

One other important thing that plants and animals had in common was the ability to reproduce themselves. To be sure, the reproduction was accomplished in different ways, but it still meant that the power of life could be handed on.

If this was what life meant, how did plants and animals use it?

In the first place, there seemed to Aristotle to be one major difference between plants and animals in the way they used their living powers. This was the power of movement. Animals could, indeed had to, move about. On the other hand, plants could exist only if they were rooted in one spot.

While plants and animals all served a purpose in the

world, their individual purposes and possibilities were quite different. Here, Aristotle concluded, it was possible to see a very definite gradation among the different kinds of living creatures. Specifically, there were three different and separate kinds of activities connected with the process of living; and, plants and animals could be put into different classes on the basis of their performing or not performing them. These activities were:

1. Nutrition and reproduction
2. Feeling
3. Reasoning and intellectual activity

1. At the lowest stage of living activity, the feature which is most characteristic of the living thing, and most important for it, is the ability to receive nourishment and to reproduce itself.

This is the function of plants. Plants do not go any farther than this. They do not respond to outside stimulation and they do not think.

2. There are, however, some living creatures that possess what in broad terms may be described as feeling; that is, the ability to perceive and to respond to something that happens to them from outside.

There are various kinds of response to outside stimulation. If you touch an earthworm, it will move. If you frighten a horse or a dog, it will run. And so on. Stimulation comes from physical contacts and also from emotions. Animals show fear, anger, hate, love, and so forth. The evidences of feeling are endless.

This capacity of feeling and responding, then, is something that is added to the power of nutrition and reproduction. It is, Aristotle concluded, the chief characteristic that distinguishes animals from plants. But it is also important to note, as Aristotle did, that the capacity of the lower stage—nutrition and reproduction—continues to exist in the next higher stage.

3. Obviously man, the highest of all animals, can do more than take in food, reproduce himself, and respond to outside stimulation. He can think, he can reason, he can engage in intellectual activity and he has the power of speech.

The power of the mind—the gift of being able to do the work of the mind—is what distinguishes man from the other animals.

Thus it was clearly the human intellect that was unique among all the things which existed in the world. True, dogs and horses—and, proverbially, elephants—can remember, can even reason on the basis of what they remember. But it is only man who has a conscious command of what is stored in his memory, and can bring back to his conscious mind whatever he wishes to remember.

Moreover, it is only man who possesses that great power called imagination which is at the basis of intellectual activity. Here, too, is included that other unique human capacity—curiosity.

Just as animals possess the characteristics of plants—notably, nutrition and reproduction—so man possesses the characteristics of all the stages of life below him. He depends upon food and can reproduce himself like the plants and animals; and he possesses feeling and responds to stimulation, just as the other animals do. In fact, it is obvious that many of the instinctive reactions of animals exist in man as well.

Such were the gradations of life, Aristotle thought, which would form a point of departure for the study of the science of life as a whole. With these abilities and functions in mind, one could begin to examine the individual creatures and see how they answered to their purpose.

◆◆

ELEVEN

The Scientist at Work

Due to Aristotle's painstaking scientific achievements, we have today the great science of biology. In addition, he founded a number of subdivisions, all of which are now separate sciences in their own right:

BOTANY—the science of plants, which Aristotle did not distinguish as a separate part of biology.

ZOOLOGY—the science of animals; again a subdivision of biology.

EMBRYOLOGY—the study of the living being as it developed from the egg. This was a wholly new science which today still preserves the form Aristotle gave it.

COMPARATIVE ANATOMY—the study of the forms and organs of animals, based on dissection.

PSYCHOLOGY—the study of the mind which to Aristotle was a natural part of biology.

ECOLOGY—the study of the effect of environment on animals.

ZOOGEOGRAPHY—the science of the distribution of animals in the various parts of the world; Aristotle was a pioneer here also.

84

How was all this vast system of biological science created? How did Aristotle found a new scientific method which was the essential preparation for all subsequent work on the subject?

If you had asked Aristotle, he would have told you quite simply that the establishment of the new science depended on two things. First, the collection of an enormous amount of evidence. Second, work patiently carried on until the evidence is all understood.

Aristotle would have said that the investigator must never give up until he is satisfied that he has made his record complete. Of course, all of Aristotle's notebooks and "laboratory notes" are lost to us, primarily because of the impossibility of preserving anything from that time written on perishable material; however, the modern scientific student can see behind his work an infinite capacity for taking pains that set the standard for all future workers in natural history.

Biology, as Aristotle had to study it, was an outdoor activity rather than a laboratory discipline. The living habits of birds and fish, as well as wild animals, all had to be observed on the spot. One had to learn where the early life of grasshoppers and gnats, for example, could be studied. Every living thing had to be traced to its home and watched there. The biologist today can work in his laboratory, but this is partly because his predecessors did their work outdoors. Also, the modern biologist can consult reference books, which Aristotle could not.

Fortunately, considering the tasks that Aristotle had to accomplish, Greece was an ideal country with an ideal climate. Today, as in Aristotle's time, the weather is sunny and bright all year around. There is some rain in the winter, but it is never heavy or continuous and the rainy spells are always punctuated by periods of sunshine. In ancient times as today, life was lived as much as possible out of doors. People were in direct touch with one another and with nature. The naturalist would never have to suspend his operations for a whole winter because of bad weather.

But it was above all in its waters—its lovely seashores, harbors, rivers, and lakes—that Greece offered ideal opportunities to the naturalist. The water of the Mediterranean has a characteristic brightness and clearness such as no other water seems to have. Indeed, on the water in Greece on a clear still day, one could watch all the marine life on the bottom and among the rocks.

How many hours, how many days, did Aristotle spend—alone or with his students—watching all the busy life that went on in the water in the lovely harbors of Assos and Mytilene? He can almost be pictured in his boat, rowed by a faithful slave or by a student. His head protected by the characteristic Greek broad-brimmed hat of linen or straw, he doubtless spent long hours leaning over the edge of the boat, peering intently into the water beneath him. Aristotle knew this marine world intimately and grew to love it.

Day by day and week by week, Aristotle studied one feature of this marine life after another. Sometimes he picked up an unexpected detail and found that it related to something else; but he had a regular program of study, and his aim was to make his notes and records complete.

There were all kinds of questions to be answered. How did the octopus reproduce? How did the lobster feed? How were the young of sharks born? Would the sponge live if detached from the rocks on which it grew? How did the different varieties of fish lay their eggs?

Year after year, on the water and on the land, the work went patiently on and the information was accumulated. Animals and plants, fish and birds were dissected and drawings made. Students were put to watching for certain things. Fishermen were consulted, and farmers and the professional hunters of birds and animals, upon whom people depended in those days for food, were questioned.

The information from all these "non-scientific" sources was brought together and digested. It had to be carefully scrutinized for errors and exaggerations. It was laborious work, but Aristotle found in it a never-ending pleasure. The more he discovered about the world of nature, the more he loved the plants with their infinite variety and secret lives of growth, the animals with their individual personalities and their domestic and social habits.

During these years of collecting and cataloging, Aristotle was lecturing all the time to his students, using his lectures —as many scientists do—to sort out his material and organize his ideas. Indeed, he depended on his students and associates for their response to his teaching, their enthusiasm, and their questions, for these meant a great deal to him.

From his students, Aristotle got an immediate return in the satisfaction and pleasure that comes to every teacher— the pleasure of seeing the students' minds grow. If his program of lifework was aimed at nothing less than the organization of all knowledge concerning the world, it was also an everyday affair which brought Aristotle and his associates into close human companionship.

The tradition goes that Aristotle's daughter helped him

with his work. We can picture the master at work with his little group of associates—including Theophrastus, his favorite pupil—and his household of slaves. Like a true Greek gentleman, Aristotle cared well for his slaves, and in his will provided that the young ones should not be sold when he died.

The Living World of Nature

The English translation of Aristotle's biological works totals something over eleven hundred large pages. It still draws naturalists to it, for these pages are filled with information that is still valid and useful. Sometimes, when Aristotle's observations escaped the attention of later scholars, his reports and conclusions were not duplicated until the nineteenth century.

Turning over the pages, one comes upon fascinating descriptions of animals and their habits. Fish, insects and mammals are cataloged, and the accounts of their lives are far from being dull reports. Aristotle was interested in everything that was alive; he knew that he could learn something from every living creature, no matter how small and undignified it might seem.

To get better acquainted with Aristotle's remarkable biological writings, let us first look at some of his pages on fish.

Fish were a major item in the diet of the ancient Greeks, and people were familiar with the different varieties. Many of the fish in Greek waters enjoyed picturesque names and even more picturesque reputations. Unique among them was the Torpedo fish which, since ancient times, has been giving electric shocks to any fish or fisherman it happens to encounter. Another remarkable fish was called the Angler fish. Both of these were common in Greek waters and every fisherman knew that they had each developed special equipment. Here is Aristotle's fascinating account:

In creatures of the sea we can find many clever devices which have been adapted to fit the circumstances of their lives. What is commonly said of the Torpedo and the Angler is indeed perfectly true.

The Torpedo, desiring to catch the other creatures on whom it lives, produces a kind of shock in its body, and so captures its victims and feeds on them. It hides in the sand and mud, and stuns all the creatures that swim by within its reach. It is even capable of causing numbness in human beings if it strikes them.

The Angler hunts its food by its own methods. It finds a place where there is plenty of mud and sand and hides itself there. This fish has a filament projecting in front of its eyes. The filament is long and thin, like a hair, and round at the tip. The Angler uses it as bait. The smaller fish, swimming about, take the filament for a piece of seaweed such as they usually eat. When the smaller fish strike at the filament, the Angler raises it and sucks them into its mouth.

The success of the Torpedo and the Angler is shown by the fact that when caught they are often found with mullet in their stomachs. They are both obviously sluggish fish, while the mullet is a fast swimmer. Thus, it is plain that this is the way they get their living.

Another indication is the fact that the Angler sometimes loses its filament, and when one of these fish with its filament missing is caught, it is thin for want of food.

Aristotle's account of the Torpedo fish is all the more remarkable because he had no knowledge of electricity. He neither knew what the effects of electricity were, nor how they were produced. But the electric shock produced an obvious reaction, and this Aristotle faithfully recorded even though it was something neither he nor anyone else at that time could explain.

The production of electricity by the Torpedo fish, as we know the fish today, is nothing uncommon. When muscle substance is contracted, it produces electricity. In the case of ordinary human muscle this is usually very slight and can be detected only by instruments. In the Torpedo, the forward part of the body contains two special muscular areas which are capable of producing electric shocks that will kill a smaller fish.

The Angler has further characteristics which have been developed in order to assist it in its manner of getting its living. It has a protective coloration which enables it to lie on the bottom and wait for its prey without being noticed. It also has an oversized head and an enormous mouth well adapted to catch the smaller fish who have been lured by the bait of the filament.

As he studied the breeding habits of these and many more creatures of the sea, Aristotle perceived how the processes of birth and raising the young had been adapted for the greatest possible protection of the young. Behind Aristotle's description of the way the octopus lays its eggs

PROPERTY OF
FRANKFORT-SCHUYLER CENTRAL
HIGH SCHOOL LIBRARY
FRANKFORT NEW YORK 13340

we can see the minute study he had devoted to the highly individual habits of this creature:

> The female octopus breeds in spring and goes into hiding for about two months. After laying her eggs, she broods over them, and this puts her in poor physical condition since during this time she does not search for food. The eggs are laid in a hole in the floor of the sea and there are so many of them that after being discharged from the mother's body, they would fill a container larger than the mother's body. The small octopuses creep out, looking like little spiders, though their limbs are not yet fully outlined. When they first leave the eggs, they are so tiny and helpless that most of them perish.

Here is Aristotle's description of the breeding habits of the catfish, also common in Greek waters:

> The catfish lays its eggs in shallow water, finding places close to roots or close to reeds. The eggs when they are laid are sticky and cling to the roots. The female catfish leaves after laying her eggs, but the male stays and watches them, driving off all other fish that might eat the eggs or the small fish when they are hatched. The male continues on guard for forty or fifty days, until the young fish are large enough to escape when they are pursued.
>
> Fishermen know when the male catfish is on guard, for when he wards off the other fish he makes a rush in the water and utters a kind of muttering sound. Having learned how conscientious the male catfish is,

fishermen drag into shallow water the plants to which the eggs are attached, and the male fish, still on guard, can then be caught with a hook. Even if he sees the hook, he will not leave his duty, and he will even bite the hook to pieces with his teeth.

In another passage Aristotle speaks of the peculiar sound produced by the catfish. He wrote, "Fish have no voice since they possess neither windpipe nor lungs, but some of them, as for example the catfish in the river Achelous (at the mouth of the Gulf of Corinth), produce sounds and squeaks by rubbing their gills."

Since the catfish known in Europe do not protect their young in the way Aristotle describes, his account was sometimes laughed at. However, in the middle of the nineteenth century the Swiss-American naturalist Louis Agassiz (1807–1873), a professor at Harvard, found that the American catfish protects its young in just the way Aristotle describes. Noticing what Aristotle had said about the catfish that live at the mouth of the Achelous River, Agassiz had some catfish from that locality sent to him. He found that they were different from the European variety and that they indeed corresponded to Aristotle's description.

Aristotle clearly brought out the fact that whales, dolphins and porpoises, though they live in the sea, are not to be classed biologically with the fish. The distinction comes in the manner of bearing and rearing their young, in which they resemble mammals. Whales, dolphins and porpoises have the characteristics of mammals in that their blood is warm and they have lungs for breathing air. The young, while they are within the mother's body, are attached to the womb by a navel string and placenta; and, they are born alive and their mothers suckle them.

What Aristotle wrote about this class of animals was important because their essential characteristics had never been fully understood before his time:

> Among the animals which bear the young alive are man, the horse, the seal and other animals that have hair, and also, among marine animals, the whale, the dolphin and the porpoise. The latter have lungs and breathe, and have a blowhole. Men have seen the dolphin asleep with his nose above the water, snoring. The dolphin and the others take in water as they feed and discharge it through the blowhole, but they also take air into their lungs.

> The young of the dolphin and the porpoise are usually born one at a time, though two are sometimes born. The young of the whale are usually born two at a time, though only one is sometimes born. The mothers produce milk and suckle the young.

> Among the dolphins the young grow rapidly, and are fully grown when ten years old. The young are born only in the summer. They accompany the parents for some time and the parents are notable for the strong affection they show their young.

As for land creatures, Aristotle devoted as much attention to the smallest and most insignificant as to the largest. For example, he had been as patient in learning the origin and growth of the gnat and the housefly as in studying any other creatures:

> Gnats grow from what are called ascarids; and ascarids are generated in the slime of wells, or in any

place in which the draining off of water has left a
moisture. This slime decays, and then turns white,
afterwards black, and finally blood-red. At this stage
there originate in it what look like tiny bits of red
weed. These at first wriggle about, clinging to one another. Finally they break loose and swim in the water;
they are now known as ascarids. After a few days they
may be seen standing straight up on the surface of the
water. At this point they are motionless and hard.
Presently the husk breaks off and the gnats, as they
now are, may be seen sitting upon it. Then the heat
of the sun, or a puff of wind, sets them in motion, and
they fly away.

In the case of all grubs and all animals that break
out of a grub state, generation is due in the first place
to the heat of the sun or to wind.

Ascarids are more often found in places in which
there is a deposit of a mixed kind, as for example in
kitchens, and in plowed fields, and they grow more
rapidly there, for the contents of such places decom-
pose more rapidly than collections of refuse elsewhere.

The cantharus or scarab beetle rolls a piece of
manure into a ball, remains hidden in it during the
winter, and gives birth inside it to small grubs, from
which the new beetles come. Flies grow from grubs in
the manure that farmers have gathered into heaps.
The grub is very small to begin with. First it takes on
a reddish color. It has up to this point been quiet, but
it now takes on a power of motion. Then it becomes
a small motionless grub. Then it moves again, and
again it returns to a motionless state. But after this
there comes out a perfect fly, and it flies away under
the influence of the sun's heat or a puff of air.

The same loving attention to detail is found in Aristotle's account of locusts and cicadas, two well-known insects of the Mediterranean landscape:

Locusts (or grasshoppers) reproduce in the same way as other insects; that is, the smaller covers the larger, for the male is smaller than the female. The females have a hollow tube in their tails. This they insert in the ground, and then lay their eggs. The male, by the way, does not have this tube.

The eggs are laid all together in one spot, so that the lump resembles a honeycomb. After they have been laid, the eggs take on the shape of oval grubs which are enveloped by a kind of thin clay, like a membrane; and inside of this membrane-like formation they grow until they are mature. The larva is so soft that it collapses at a touch. The larva is not placed in the surface of the ground, but a little below the surface. When it reaches maturity, it emerges from its clay-like covering as a little black grasshopper, and it gradually grows larger.

The eggs are laid at the close of the summer and the grasshopper dies after laying them. The male grasshopper dies at about the same time. In springtime the young grasshoppers come out of the ground. Since the eggs are laid in cracks of the soil, grasshoppers are not found in mountains or in poor soil, but only in flat and crumbly land. The eggs remain in the ground during the winter and when summer comes last year's larva develops into a perfect grasshopper.

There are two kinds of cicadas. One, which is small, is the first to come and the last to disappear. The other is the large variety, which sings; and this comes last and disappears first. But some of the small cicadas which are divided at the waist can sing.

The cicada is not found in places where there are no trees; but it is found in quantity in places where there are olive trees, for an olive grove does not have thick shade. It does not live in cold places, and is not found in any grove that keeps out the sunlight.

The cicadas lay their eggs in uncultivated soil, depositing them in a hole bored by a pointed organ they carry in the rear, like locusts. They also lay their eggs in the hollow canes with which farmers prop up vines. They perforate these canes and lay their eggs in them. The larva runs into the ground. The grub reaches its full size in the ground and becomes what is called a "nymph," and it is at this stage that the creature is sweetest to the taste, before the husk is broken. In the middle of the summer, the creature comes out of its husk during the night, and in a moment, as the husk breaks, the larva becomes a perfect cicada. At once the creature turns black in color and becomes harder and larger; and it now begins to sing. It is the male that sings, while the female has no voice. At first the males are sweeter to eat; but when the females are reproducing and are full of eggs they are sweeter to eat.

If you offer your finger to a cicada, and bend back the tip of the finger, and then offer it again, it will be more responsive than if you were to keep your finger outstretched all the while. It will then set about climbing your finger, for its eyesight is so weak that it will climb your finger as though it were a moving leaf.

These are only samples of the enormous collection of minute and accurate information gathered in Aristotle's books on animals. If we remember how primitive his tools and instruments were, we realize how strong his drive for knowledge must have been.

Moreover, all that Aristotle knew he had to find out for himself. He was the first to classify birds scientifically, counting approximately 170 varieties of them. He was the first to catalog fishes, and listed 110 kinds, with descriptions of their bodily structure, food, breeding habits, migrations, and the way they were caught. He listed 120 invertebrate creatures—that is, animals or fish that lack a backbone or spine.

Many of these animals Aristotle dissected, as we can see from his descriptions of them. Modern anatomists have determined the following list of creatures he must have opened and studied:

Mammals	Birds	Reptiles	Fish	Invertebrates
Bat	Chicken	Chameleon	Conger	Crab
Deer	Dove	Frog	Dogfish	Cuttlefish
Dolphin	Duck	Grass snake	Eel	Lobster
Elephant	Goose	Lizard	Mullet	Locust
Hare	Owl	Toad	Stargazer	Octopus
Horse	Partridge	Tortoise		Sea urchin
Mole	Pigeon			Snail
Mouse	Quail			
Ox	Swan			
Pig				
Weasel				

It seems certain that Aristotle never dissected a human body, although he describes the bones of the human head quite fully. The Greeks of his day had a special aversion to leaving bodies unburied, and the dead were laid away as soon as possible. Thus it is not surprising that Aristotle was not able to make this type of dissection.

This research in natural science, together with the work to be described in later chapters, covers the whole of Aristotle's life. It is not possible for us to say that he did his biological work at one time in one place, his political research at another time and in another place, and so on. So far as historians can tell, he was actively engaged in all areas of research at all times throughout his life—which makes his accomplishments even more amazing.

The Beginning of Life

If Aristotle had done nothing else, he would have been famous today as the founder of the science of embryology. This highly important and practical specialty studies the development of life from the egg—human or animal—and traces all the complicated stages in the life of the embryo, that is, the young animal before it emerges from the egg or the womb to start its own life.

What Aristotle's work has meant to later scientists is illustrated by the opinion of the English scholar George Henry Lewes (1817–1878). One of the most penetrating philosophical writers of his day, Lewes had this to say about Aristotle's work on embryology:

> It is an extraordinary production. No ancient work, and few modern works, equal it in comprehensiveness of detail and profound speculative insight. We find there some of the obscurest problems of biology treated with a mastery which, when we consider the condition of science at that day, is truly astounding.

Aristotle was fascinated by the process of the development of all life during its earliest stages. Today his observations are still valid and still set standards for biologists. Moreover, what he discovered is not only purely scientific knowledge, but also practical information for both physicians and farmers.

Here is Aristotle's account of the embryo of the chick which is still the classic description among biologists and physicians:

Generation from the egg proceeds in the same manner with all birds, but the full periods from conception to birth differ. In the case of the ordinary hen, the first indication of the embryo appears after three days and three nights. The interval is longer with larger birds, shorter with smaller birds. In the meantime the yolk has come into being, rising toward the pointed end of the egg, where the egg is hatched. The heart appears first, like a speck of blood, in the white of the egg.

This point beats and moves as though it possessed life. From it there begin to grow two vein-ducts carrying blood. A membrane carrying bloody fibers now envelops the yolk. A little afterwards the body begins to take shape, at first very small and white. The head is clearly distinguished, and the eyes are swollen out to a great extent. This condition of the eyes lasts for a good while, for it is only gradually that they become smaller. At the beginning the lower portion of the body is insignificant compared with the upper portion.

When the egg is ten days old the chick and all its parts are clearly visible. The head is still larger than the rest of the body. The eyes are larger than the head, but they do not yet possess the power of sight. If the eyes are removed at this time, they are seen to be larger than beans, and black. If the cuticle is peeled off them, there is a white and cold liquid inside, which glitters in the sunlight; but there is no hard substance at all.

At this time also the larger internal organs are visible, as are also the stomach and the arrangement of the viscera. The veins that seem to proceed from the heart are now close to the navel.

The disposition of the several parts is as follows. First, on the outside, comes the membrane of the egg, not that of the shell, but underneath it. Inside this membrane is a white liquid. Then comes the chick, with a membrane around it, separating it so as to keep the chick free of the liquid. Next after the chick comes the yolk.

About the twentieth day, if you open the egg and touch the chick, it moves inside and chirps. It is already coming to be covered with down when, after the twentieth day is past, the chick begins to break the shell. The head is situated over the right leg close to the flank, and the wing is placed over the head. By and by the yolk, diminishing gradually in size, at length becomes entirely used up and included within the chick. During this period the chick sleeps, wakes up, makes a move, and looks up and chirps. The heart and the navel together palpitate as though the creature were breathing.

Birds lay some eggs that are unfruitful, and no life comes from such eggs by incubation; and this phenomenon is observed especially with pigeons.

Twin eggs have two yolks. In some twin eggs a thin partition of white intervenes to prevent the yolks mixing with each other, but some twin eggs are unprovided with such a partition, and the yolks run into one another. A hen has been known to lay eighteen eggs, and to hatch twins out of them all, except those that were wind-eggs; the rest were fertile—though, by the way, one of the twins was always bigger than the other—but the eighteenth was abnormal.

Aristotle and his helpers doubtless spent long and patient hours working with chickens. A considerable number of eggs had to be collected as soon as laid, then dated, and carefully preserved, to be opened in succession, each at exactly the right time. How, for example, did these busy embryologists come to discover the special powers of the hen who laid so many twin eggs? Did Aristotle perhaps in the end dissect her in an effort to discover the cause of so many twins? At any rate, this Greek hen has become immortal in the pages of Aristotle.

And, out of such study came these important results:

1. Aristotle showed for the first time that the unfertilized egg is a highly complicated mechanism with many different parts, all waiting to perform their predetermined functions. These functions all begin at the moment when fertilization occurs.

2. Earlier scientists had never been able to discover at what point in the development of the embryo the sex of the creature was determined. Aristotle proved that the differentiation into male or female took place at the very beginning of the embryo.

3. Aristotle discovered for the first time what the real function of the placenta and of the umbilical cord were.

4. By introducing the comparative method—that is, by studying and comparing the embryos of different types of animals—Aristotle was able to show more clearly the significance of the development of each type of embryo.

5. One of Aristotle's most useful contributions was to demonstrate that as the embryo developed, the general characteristics of the creature appeared before the specific characteristics.

6. Aristotle anticipated modern studies by his emphasis on the development of the heart and the vascular (carried by veins) system in the embryo. He made the important observation that the heart is the first part of the body to live and the last to die.

Here, then, was a new science which has played an important part in the daily life of mankind ever since Aristotle opened his eggs. Indeed, Aristotle's work on embryology has lasted as a body of knowledge that has never been proved inaccurate.

◆◆◆

FOURTEEN

The Ladder of Life

When one surveys the whole picture of the plant and animal world, the first thing he realizes is that there are many ways in which plants and animals are interrelated. There are relationships of shape and similarities of activity. Some plants resemble each other in structure, and many animals have the same organs, or similar parts.

As he worked at his dissections and built up his records, it became clear to Aristotle that plants and animals could be grouped into classes. Out of this grouping, he hoped, something very exciting might come; namely, might not the groups and classes be the key to understanding how plants and animals had come to be what they were?

The basis of Aristotle's classification was the structure of the plant or the animal. It was the structure that determined what the plant or animal did in the world of nature, and set it off from other plants and animals.

So it was that Aristotle began to look carefully for both resemblances and differences among his plants and animals. However, he also realized that simply working out a system and a classification was not enough. It would not serve its purpose unless one understood exactly what it meant.

105

Therefore, Aristotle began to develop in his mind a kind of checklist of points that would have definite meaning:

1. The parts and limbs of animals; what they were and what their special characteristics were.
2. The organs and their structure.
3. The functions of the parts and organs.
4. The method of reproduction.
5. Signs of inherited characteristics.
6. How the embryo develops.
7. How the young are born and cared for.
8. Diseases.
9. The effect of environment.
10. Evidence for the animal's psychology and for the extent of its intelligence.

In addition, as a working rule, Aristotle established three grades of likeness in the plant and animal world:

1. The *species,* such as man, the domestic horse, and so on. The species is a group of animals or plants, all of which have one or more characteristics that set them off from other similar groups. The members of a species breed with one another and the offspring have the parents' characteristics. One might call the species the smallest possible group which can be divided into other groups.

2. The second, and larger classification is the *genus.* Genus is the Greek word meaning "kind" or "race." For example, the horse belongs to a genus which includes donkeys and zebras, which have features in common with the horse but also are different from it in important ways.

3. Above the genus Aristotle grouped what he called the *larger genus,* which biologists today would sometimes

call the *family*. Such a family would be the mammals, which nurse their young.

Aristotle did not set up as many classifications as scientists have since found necessary, but his bases for making divisions have remained valid. Today we work in terms of the following classifications:

Aristotle	*Modern Categories*
1. Species	1. Species: for example, collie dogs.
2. Genus	2. Genus: all dogs, wolves, jackals, etc.
3. Larger genus	3. Family: the foregoing, plus foxes, etc.
	4. Order: all meat-eating animals, such as dogs, foxes, wolves, jackals, cats, weasels, hyenas, etc.
	5. Class: mammals, including the foregoing plus men, cows, elephants, mice, bats, whales, etc.
	6. Phylum: all vertebrates (animals possessing a backbone).

Aristotle's groups enabled him to set apart and study what seemed to be the most significant characteristics of each group of animals and plants. As he himself wrote, none of his predecessors had tried to determine why a certain kind of animal had a certain type of limb or organ, and what effect this particular limb or organ had on the animal's life.

Actually Aristotle's own words best illustrate the way he reasoned:

> Nature's original and special way of working is to employ the parts which are common to all animals in such a way as to reach special ends. For example, in the case of the mouth, all animals use it to receive their food, but only some of them use it as a weapon of attack and defense. Other animals use the mouth for speech. Nor do all animals use it for breathing. But nature has combined all these functions into one instrument, and it has made the mouth different in different animals, according to different requirements. Thus, some animals have large mouths, some small ones. The animals that use the mouth for food, breathing and speech have small mouths. Those that use it as a weapon and a means of protection have great jaws and teeth. Since their safety depends upon their ability to bite, it is better for them to have a mouth with a large opening. The wider the mouth can open, the better they can bite. The fish that bite, or eat other fish, have large mouths, while other fish have small mouths. Birds in the same way have what we call the beak for a mouth, and the beak to a bird is what the lips and teeth are to other animals. And among birds the beak differs in size and use according to its use by the bird.

Horns and tusks show the same kind of adaptation to the needs of the animal. About these Aristotle writes:

No animal that has fingers or anything resembling fingers has horns. With fingers, it has other means of defense than horns. Indeed nature has supplied some animals with claws, some with teeth, others with other parts which can be used for protection. The animals to which nature has not given horns have other means of saving themselves. For example, swiftness is the horse's protection, while size is the protection of the camel or the elephant against the attacks of other animals. Stags, antelopes and gazelles are furnished with both speed and horns. They defend themselves from certain animals by means of their horns, from other animals by means of their speed.

The human hand, Aristotle points out, is one of the highest developments in all animal life:

The hand is not one tool, but many. It is, as it were, the greatest of all tools. All other animals have but one tool, that is, one weapon of defense, and they cannot exchange it for another. The animal has to do everything that he does with this one tool, and an animal of this kind can never give up its constant care and watchfulness, and it can never get another kind of tool.

But man, with his hand, has a variety of means of preserving and defending himself, and he can always change these means. He can use any weapon he chooses, and he can use it whenever he wishes to do so. His hand is both nail and claw and horn, and he can also use a spear or sword, or any other tool or weapon.

In terms of the animal kingdom as a whole, what did this mean? To Aristotle, it meant:

1. That living things were interconnected and related with one another structurally;
2. That they possessed some of each other's characteristics; and
3. That some plants and animals had come to have a higher stage of development than others.

These highest forms, so to speak, could do more than the lower forms. They could do more complicated things, and they could play a greater part in the world of nature and the world of animals.

At the top of the scale, of course, was man, who could do things that no other animal could do. Aristotle wrote down his understanding of this in a passage that has become famous in biological literature:

Nature proceeds little by little from lifeless things to animal life, in such a way that it is impossible to determine the exact line of demarcation; and it is impossible to determine on which side of this line certain organisms lie. In the upward scale, lifeless things are followed by plants, and plants will differ from one another because they seem to have different amounts of life. Thus, plants as a whole do not possess life—that is, strength and motion—as compared with an animal; but plants do possess life if they are compared with lifeless things.

Indeed, one can observe in plants a continuous scale of ascent toward the animal. In the sea one can find certain objects which it is difficult to establish as either animal or vegetable. For instance, certain of these are well rooted, and will perish if they are detached from their roots. In these respects a sponge completely resembles a plant, for throughout its life it is attached to a rock, and if it is separated from the rock it dies.

Slightly different from the sponges are what are called "sea-lungs," and various other animals that resemble them. These are free and unattached, but they have no feeling, and their life is simply that of a plant separated from the ground.

Even among land plants there are some that are independent of the soil, or even entirely free. There is a plant found on Mount Parnassus which will live for a considerable time if you hang it up on a peg. Some of the mollusks or slugs, for instance, and similar organisms resemble plants in that they never live unattached to something. On the other hand, since they possess a certain flesh-like substance, they must be supposed to have some degree of feeling.

The sea-nettles lie outside the recognized groups. Their constitution, like that of some of the mollusks and slugs, makes them resemble plants in some ways, animals in others. Since some of them can detach themselves and can fasten on their food, and since they move when objects come into contact with them, they have at least something of an animal nature. This is also indicated by the way in which they can use the hard parts of their bodies as a protection against enemies. On the other hand they are closely allied to plants in several ways. Their structure is imperfect and does not resemble an animal structure. They are able to attach themselves to rocks, and do this with great speed; and although they possess a mouth, they do not produce excreta.

In another famous passage, Aristotle goes on to write:

Nature passes from lifeless objects to animals in unbroken sequence, putting between them organisms which live but are not animals. In the matter of being able to feel, some animals give no indication of it, while others indicate it in an indistinct way. The substance of some of these intermediate creatures is flesh-like; but the sponge is in every respect like a vegetable.

And so throughout the entire animal scale there is a gradual difference in amount of vitality and in the ability to move. The same is true with regard to habits of life. Thus, in the case of plants that grow from seed, the one function of the plant seems to be the reproduction of its own particular species. In the same way, the action of certain animals is similarly limited.

The faculty of reproduction, then, is common to all living things. If you add the capacity for feeling, then their lives will differ from one another in respect to methods of reproduction, modes of giving birth, and ways of raising the young. Some animals, like plants, merely reproduce their own species at definite seasons. Other animals keep themselves busy obtaining food for their young, but after the young have grown up, the parents abandon them and have nothing more to do with them. Other animals are more intelligent and possess the ability to remember, and these live with their offspring for a longer period and on a basis more resembling human society.

Thus the Ladder of Life, or the Tree of Life, as Aristotle conceived it, would show an upward progression, something like this:

Man

Mammals, divided into hairy four-footed animals, or land mammals, and whales, dolphins, and porpoises, or sea mammals. Aristotle was the first to realize that whales and other sea mammals were related in structure and function to land mammals

Birds

Reptiles and amphibious animals (toads, frogs, newts, and salamanders)

Fishes

Squid, cuttlefish, octopuses

Water-breathing animals with jointed limbs, such as lobsters, shrimps, and crabs

Creatures with the body divided into segments, such as insects and spiders

Other shellfish with soft bodies protected by shells, such as snails, clams, and oysters

Jellyfish

Sponges

Higher forms of plants

Lower forms of plants

Inanimate matter

Aristotle's Ladder of Life or, in Latin, *scala naturae,* remained for a long time the chief basis for all biological study. Within that scale, Aristotle showed that there were certain general characteristics which distinguished certain groups, and these distinctions seemed to indicate an ascent from lower to higher forms. For example, there was the question of whether a creature possessed blood or not, and here the division resulted as follows:

A. CREATURES WITH BLOOD
   Man
   Mammals
   Birds
   Reptiles and amphibious creatures
   Fishes
B. CREATURES WITHOUT BLOOD
   Squid, etc.
   Lobsters, etc.
   Insects, spiders
   Other shellfish
   Jellyfish
   Sponges

There was also a significant difference in the way the young were born. In the case of man and the mammals, the young were born alive and independent, while in other cases the young were born in eggs or (in the case of insects) from worms.

Another important difference in classification was between the vertebrates (animals with a backbone or skeleton) and the invertebrates (animals without skeleton or backbone). The vertebrates are man, mammals, birds, reptiles, amphibious creatures and fishes. All other organisms are invertebrates.

Just how permanent was Aristotle's vast scheme of classifying plants and animals? As a matter of fact, it remained the basis for all subsequent work, down to modern times. True, during the Middle Ages some of his information was overlooked. For example, the fact that whales, dolphins and porpoises are mammals was not rediscovered until the 1500's. Moreover, today's classification of the birds is still not perfect, and Aristotle's grouping remained the one in use until quite recent times. In the classification of fishes, his separation of those with bones and those with cartilege is still used; obviously Aristotle could only have made this observation on the basis of the most careful dissection. In addition, his distinction between shellfish, sponges and jellyfish is still valuable; indeed, the classification today is much as he left it.

If one were to ask in what specific aspect of biology Aristotle made his most important contribution, the answer would be that branch of science we now call *organology*—the study of the organs of plants and animals. Aristotle devoted special care to the organs because in them he saw the clearest and most important evidence for the development of animals and their adaptation to their environment.

Also under organology, modern scientists include *morphology*, which is the study of the form and structure of animals and plants, and *physiology*, which is the study of the function of the organs.

So Aristotle's work went on—dissection, comparison,

classification. Slowly the meaning of all the material began to become clear. Surely, he thought, the ladder of life meant that there was an upward movement, a scale of improvement of some kind. Yet how had this come about and what did it mean?

What Was Evolution?

Everything that Nature makes is a means to an end," wrote Aristotle. "For just as human creations are the products of art, in the same way living objects are plainly the products of a comparable cause or principle. If we believe that heaven was brought into being and is maintained by such a cause, then we have more reason to believe that mortal animals originated in this way."

These were the words in which Aristotle set down the philosophy that his study of biology had led him to. Was he in fact contemplating the notion of evolution, somewhat along the lines of Charles Darwin's famous theory? Indeed there is much in Aristotle's work that seems to point in that direction.

The theory of evolution was put forward by Darwin in his famous book the *Origin of Species,* published in 1859. While other scientists before him had come upon indications of the same idea, it was Darwin who put it into its final form—namely, the discovery that living things, both plants and animals, have their origins in other, lower, forms of life. By changes occurring in successive generations, a plant or animal is modified and develops into a higher form.

Scientists have shown that the trend of these evolutionary changes and developments is normally from a lower to a higher form. A simple plant or animal develops into something more complicated, with greater capacities and a greater role to play in the world.

In this way, students of evolution believe, all anim ls and plants have descended ultimately from a few v ry simple organisms. In fact, modern research is beginning to show that there was indeed at the start one original organism. This might have been similar to the simplest protozoans that we know today.

However, some types of living creatures that came into being in this way have now ceased to exist. If these types, and the others which still exist, are compared and their connections traced, the result will be a kind of family tree. This tree will show how some types branched out from the main trunk and then ceased to develop further, while other types have continued to change.

In all such changes, biologists see the effect of heredity, variation and natural selection. When a plant or animal happens to be different in structure or physical characteristics from its parent stock, it may prove to be the ancestor of a new type.

As plants and animals live and reproduce themselves, the process of "natural selection," resulting in "the survival of the fittest," plays its part. This means that those plants and animals will survive which are best fitted to the environment in which they live. If the chance variation in one individual happens to make it more fit to survive, then that individual represents the beginning of a new and improved type.

That these changes, called *mutations,* occur, either gradually or suddenly, is a well-established fact. The process is familiar not only to students of biology but to breeders and trainers of animals, and gardeners who notice the development of flowers.

The modern understanding of evolution goes back to a number of scientists who worked in the middle and late 1700's. One was the English physician and poet Erasmus Darwin (1731–1802), grandfather of Charles, and another was the French naturalist, the Count de Buffon (1707–1788). Buffon was noted for his eloquent descriptions of animals and natural phenomena in general. In particular, he pointed out the influence which the development of animal organs exerted on the character of different species of animals. The earlier Darwin, in his works on nature, anticipated his grandson's work by hinting that all animals had a common ancestor.

Working at the same time as Buffon was the Swedish botanist Linnaeus (1707–1778), who drew up a modern scientific system for classification.

These men were followed by the great French naturalist, Jean Baptiste Lamarck (1744–1829). Lamarck observed that changes in environment produce changes in animals and plants, establishing this as a fact that must be taken into account in any biological work. For example, the giraffe developed a long neck because he wanted to be able to eat the leaves of tall trees; and the duck developed webbed feet because he attempted to swim. Thus the giraffe became different from other quadrupeds, and the duck different from land birds.

A little later, another Frenchman, Baron Cuvier (1769–1832), working only a short time before Darwin himself, began his studies and put the science of comparative anatomy into its final form.

On the basis of the work of his predecessors, plus his

own study and reflection, Charles Darwin produced his theory of evolution by adding his own idea of "natural selection." Thus, mankind has come to a new understanding of the origin and development of life, including the physical origin of the human race.

In Aristotle's work is there any hint, any conception of such a process of evolution? Could a profound and original thinker such as Aristotle come upon such an idea with the material available to him in his time?

The astonishingly close connection between some kinds of animals must have been obvious to Aristotle as well as to other investigators. Just as many members of the animal kingdom resemble each other, so many of them have obvious things in common with man. In Aristotle's time and before the daily life of Greek households had been enlivened by pet monkeys, the most familiar variety of which was the tailless Barbary ape. In fact, he calls attention to the monkey's obvious similarities to human beings.

For Aristotle, there was a lesson here that could not be missed. The ladder of life showed there was a definite rising scale in living things, progressing from the simplest plants to men. The question was: What was the meaning of the successive changes in this rising scale? Were the changes designed? Or were they the result of some necessity coming from the environment of the plant or animal?

Aristotle found the answer in what could be seen in the organism, that is, the individual living being. As the organism—the individual—grows, it changes continually from a simple form to a more complicated one.

What, then, is the significance of such changes?

They show, Aristotle thought, that among animals every form and shape of body is the result of the body being adapted to the kind of work it has to do. Everything in nature exists for the sake of something else. Plants serve to feed animals, animals live by feeding on each other and on plants, man feeds on both plants and other animals.

Every animal was shaped and adapted for the sort of role it played in the natural world and for the way it had to live. Nature suited her tools to the work, not the work to the tools. Nothing in nature is isolated or without a purpose. This last thought was the basis of all Aristotle's studies of organisms.

Moreover, to Aristotle, the differences that could be observed among animals showed how structure was determined by function. The shape of a bird's wing was given to the wing by the fact that it was used for flying. The fish's fins and tail were shaped as they were because the fish swam in water. Aristotle wrote that "if any one part of any importance changes, the whole structure of the animal becomes very different."

Aristotle's conclusion comes very close to Darwin's theory. But Aristotle stopped short of Darwin, for he only studied the effect of the change on the animal, and did not undertake to explain the process by which the change was effected. Aristotle explained the "why" but not the "how."

Darwin was able to go further than Aristotle because Darwin's predecessors had all been working in the same direction, and above all because Darwin had the geological evidence for the early stages in the origin and development of plant and animal life. Yet in the end, Darwin agreed with Aristotle that all plant and animal structure represents the result of adaptation, and that the structure of animals especially is to be explained on the basis of usefulness.

There was another respect in which Darwin was able to go beyond Aristotle, and this was in recognizing that evolution was a historical fact. True, Aristotle had showed that evolution was a logical development which one could expect in nature, and which served a good purpose. But Darwin, with more experimental information available to him than Aristotle had, was able to prove not only that evolution was a logical development, but that it actually had occurred in history. It was a fact that had taken place in time.

Yet, if Aristotle was held back by the limitations of science in his own day, he did go beyond Darwin and Darwin's contemporaries in the matter of the philosophical explanation of evolution. Before Aristotle's time, the Greek point of view was that science was investigated on the basis of reason and philosophy, rather than as an experimental undertaking. Aristotle introduced the objective method, based on the collection of verified data, and this changed the future of science. At the same time, however, the philosophical point of view remained dominant. This was where Aristotle differed from Darwin.

To Aristotle, evolution was not, as it was to Darwin, a main interest and goal, forming a new contribution to scientific thought. Evolution, to Aristotle, was but one branch of the total knowledge of the universe. This total sum of knowledge included everything that man could know about the heavens, the earth, man in all his aspects, and all the world of nature. As a Greek philosopher, Aristotle was obliged to take all of these subjects within his field of interest and activity.

This meant that to Aristotle the ladder of life involved far more than just a scale of physical progression and improvement. The implications of evolution were not merely physical; they included every aspect of the living world.

Thus, if one began by investigating the structure and parts of animals and plants, and their methods of reproduction, one must also consider—especially in the case of animals—their manner of life, customs, habits, social organization, and so on. Here one must study whatever it is that animals have that might correspond to the intellect and the soul in man.

Therefore, when Aristotle in his organization of knowledge came to consider man, he studied not only man's physical structure and its relation to the structure of other animals, but he also studied man with respect to his manners, customs, character and morals. And, in this way, the comparative study would show how far man has risen above the other animals.

Thus it was that Aristotle, together with his biological treatises, composed philosophical works on mankind's habits of life and society (the books, *Ethics* and *Politics*); on man's thinking and reasoning power (*Logic*); on what man has done in language and rhetoric (*Rhetoric* and *Poetics*); and on his productive activity.

This whole study of man was based on the biological conception of an ascending development in human life and thought, matching the ascent which could be traced in the study of other forms of life. Hence, to Aristotle, the idea of evolution, through plants and animals to man, was the idea of advance and development toward an end. And this end—as illustrated by man's achievements—was good.

The New School in Athens

Outside the walls of Athens, northeast of the city between the Ilissus River and Mount Lycabettus, there was a grove of trees that had for many years been sacred to Apollo and the Muses. The god Apollo, who was worshiped here, was called Apollo Lyceius, because of the legend that he had come from Lycia in Asia Minor. Within the grove there were two marble temples—one dedicated to Apollo, the other to the Muses.

All around Athens there were sacred groves where the Athenians loved to walk in the cool shade of the trees and converse. The grove of Apollo and the Muses had been one of the favorite resorts of Socrates, who walked here surrounded by his friends. It was characteristic of Socrates that although he was one of the greatest teachers in Athens, he had no school; his school was wherever he and his friends happened to be.

It was near this very grove that Aristotle, when he returned to Athens after his thirteen-year absence, decided to establish a school and research center. People called the grove the Lyceum, after Apollo's title, and this name was also given to Aristotle's school, which became one of the most famous centers of learning the world has ever known.

It was not however as Plato's successor that Aristotle was returning. In fact, he had no desire to have any association with Plato's Academy. His work had taken him into a different path of inquiry and he could not feel at home in the Academy which now, under another head, had other interests than his own.

In addition, Aristotle was now very likely thinking that it was time to make a change in his environment. He was fifty years old, an age at which many scientists and scholars find their work is coming to full maturity. To bring it to completion, he needed more students and assistants than he could gather around himself at Stagira. Also, he increasingly felt the necessity of training successors who would carry on his work.

Theophrastus, who had been with Aristotle since Assos, came with the master and assisted him greatly in establishing the new school.

At first the master met his students in the covered public walk, called the *peripatos,* which had been built at the grove to provide shelter from sun and rain. Walks of this kind—consisting of nothing more than a double row of columns, supporting a roof—were common in ancient Greece. They allowed friends to stroll up and down under shelter while at the same time, since the structure had no sides, they could enjoy the open air.

On other days Aristotle's group would meet in one of the covered colonnades which ran all around the walls of the two temples in the grove. In the mild Athenian winter these porches caught the warmth of the sun and provided shelter from the wind.

In the outdoor life of Greece it was a traditional method of teaching for the master to walk slowly up and down, followed by his pupils who would listen and ask questions as the little party leisurely made its way from one end of the walk or temple porch to the other. From this custom, Aristotle's followers became known as the *Peripatetics*— "people who walk up and down."

As the group grew, it was necessary to have some kind of permanent headquarters, for Aristotle wished to have his fine collection of books, maps and his scientific specimens available to his students. But Aristotle had been born in Stagira, not Athens, and, as a non-Athenian, he was prohibited by law from purchasing property in Athens. Instead he had to rent some buildings in the neighborhood of the grove.

With enough room now at his disposal, Aristotle could expand his activities, and the routine of the school was soon established. The mornings were spent with the regular pupils, in lectures or advanced discussions on technical subjects. This work finished, Aristotle would give public lectures in the afternoon or evening. In these, he suited his treatment to the more general audience of the beginning students and the Athenians who came out from the city to hear him. Sometimes there were lectures given by the senior assistants, such as the faithful Theophrastus.

All this while, Aristotle continued to work on his scientific records. The pupils helped in the research, sometimes working with the master, sometimes with the "scholarchs" or assistant teachers whose task it was to guide the new pupils through introductory studies.

Over the years Aristotle had collected a large library; it was, in fact, a remote forerunner of the great university libraries and public libraries of later times. In those days, when all books had to be copied out by hand, it was by no means an easy task to build up a library. Sometimes a scholar had to search for some time, even write letters to friends in cities all over the Greek world, before he could locate a certain book of which he wished a copy made. Then a reliable scribe had to be engaged, and special arrangements had to be made for sending the book to its owner. For there was no postal service then and the transportation of anything so valuable as a handwritten book had to be entrusted to travelers and ship captains.

Since it was so difficult to procure books, a large library such as Aristotle's was all the more precious. The same was true of his irreplaceable notes and scientific records, along with the unique collection of laboratory specimens, with which Aristotle illustrated his lectures. Alexander the Great, who well knew the value of all this material, sent his old tutor a generous gift of money to help install the books and specimens in proper quarters.

Alexander not only provided funds for the new school, but also gave orders that all fishermen and hunters throughout his empire—and it was by now becoming a very large one—should send in reports of anything they saw that was of unusual scientific interest. And of course the scientific staff attached to Alexander's army continued to send interesting specimens to Aristotle.

The students had their meals together, and once a month there was a "symposium," or general social meeting and dinner attended by all members of the group, at which there was a discussion of some subject of general interest.

The buildings of the Lyceum corresponded quite closely with those of a modern college or university. There was a chapel, with statues of the Graces and of the great men who had been associated with the school. There were lecture rooms, a dining hall, a library, studies for the members of the faculty, rooms for the students, gardens, walks and cloisters.

There are passages in Aristotle's lectures in which he mentions various details of his own lecture room. Indeed, it must have been very much like a typical lecture room in in a modern college. There was a three-legged table, a bronze globe, a wooden sofa, and some statues of historical figures. On the walls there were tablets giving lists of the virtues and the vices, which were used to illustrate lectures on social subjects. There were tables of the animal and vegetable species for use in the scientific lectures. Also written up on the walls were illustrations of logical reasoning, designed to show how arguments were to be developed and scientific conclusions were to be reached. Anatomical diagrams and maps stood around the walls pinned to boards.

Instead of writing in white chalk on black boards, it was the custom in ancient Greece to write in charcoal on a wooden board painted white.

The lecture room also contained a famous painting, a picture of Socrates in prison on the last day of his life. Socrates was shown sitting on his bed surrounded by his friends, who were allowed to visit him. This was a reminder of Plato's celebrated account of the death of Socrates. Plato related how the great man spent his last day on earth discussing with his friends the proofs that the wise man will look upon the approach of death with cheerful confidence.

As he spoke in his lecture room, Aristotle often referred to the drawings and diagrams on the walls. The biological drawings were marked at various points of reference with the letters of the Greek alphabet. Aristotle made frequent use of such drawings in his teaching, and he was the first biologist to illustrate his books with drawings.

With a little imagination we can in fact "hear" the voice of Aristotle as he spoke in his lecture room. For it is plain from their contents that some of his preserved writings are his own notes, prepared as guides for his lectures. Every student and teacher will recognize these as typical lecture outlines. The professor repeats what he has said in other lectures, or earlier in the same lecture. Or he corrects his former statements. Sometimes in these notes he adds to what he has already written elsewhere, or occasionally in the margin he marks a passage to be omitted from the lecture.

Most of Aristotle's writings, including these rough lecture notes, were carefully preserved after his death. Copied and recopied by successive generations of scribes until the time when printing was invented, they have come down to us essentially in the same form in which Aristotle himself wrote and used them.

Aristotle's Lyceum was more or less an informal gathering of students and teachers. In fact, they referred to each other as "friends." There was no fixed number of years that a student had to attend, no prescribed course of lectures, no examinations, no degrees, no diplomas. Students came and went according to their interests and their financial means. Sometimes a student would have to leave the school for a time, but then would be able to return later. Moreover, the students paid fees according to their ability and sometimes a wealthy parent would make a present to the endowment of the school. Alumni sent gifts when they could.

Yet with all its informality, the Lyceum amounted to what would be called a university today—a community of students and teachers dedicated to the study of all branches of knowledge, and engaged in advancing and enlarging knowledge. One of the essentials of the modern university —the combination of study, teaching and research—was also one of the basic ideas of Aristotle's program.

Unlike modern teaching methods, however, it was the Greek tradition for knowledge to be transmitted orally— by direct contact between teacher and pupil. The written word, preserved in a book which could be put aside and perhaps forgotten or misinterpreted, was held to be of much less importance than the personal relationship between master and disciple. Schools such as Plato's and Aristotle's offered ideal settings for this personal and informal handing on of the tradition. Indeed, the simple life of Athens in those days was the perfect background for the leisurely life of student and teacher alike.

S E V E N T E E N

The Sum of Knowledge

In his school at Athens, Aristotle set out to organize all of his scientific work. In addition to his many biological works, he wrote on physics, astronomy, psychology, moral conduct, political science, education and literary style. The complete English translation of his works fills twelve large volumes, of which two are on biology. Few men indeed of later times ever attempted to master so many of the branches of human knowledge.

While Aristotle's biology set the standard for all later work and is still useful today, the story of his accomplishments in astronomy and physics is quite different. Without precise instruments, and having no real knowledge of chemistry as we know it, he was far more limited than in biology. Thus his conclusions in these other sciences inevitably remained more theoretical than practical.

Aristotle was forced, for example, to work with the old concept that the four basic elements of matter were earth, air, fire, and water, and that out of these the entire universe was formed. This is as far as what might be called his "chemistry" went. With only this theory to go on—and an incorrect one at that—he was naturally prohibited from certain further discoveries in physics and chemistry. Yet it must be remembered that it was not until the time of the English investigator, Robert Boyle (1627–1691), that chemistry became an independent science and the nature of the chemical elements began to be understood.

Despite these handicaps, however, Aristotle did comprehend very well what it was that needed to be explained and understood in these fields. What was the origin of motion and how was motion imparted from one object to another? What is the origin of life and what is the cause of growth? These were some of the basic questions for which he sought answers. Indeed, some still remain to be found by modern scientists.

Aristotle's theory of astronomy was that the earth was a stationary sphere surrounded by hollow spheres which revolved around the earth. In these hollow spheres were placed the moon, the sun, the five known planets and the fixed stars. In this scheme, the heaven of the fixed stars was the outermost circle of the world.

As a part of his study of meteorology—the science of the atmosphere and its phenomena—Aristotle attempted to discover the interaction of the elements of nature and the causes of such phenomena as thunder, winds, rain, snow, comets, dew, earthquakes, lightning, rainbows, and storms.

In addition, Aristotle sought to understand the ideas of space, time, continuity, infinity. In geometry, Aristotle used the knowledge then current concerning lines and circles, which in the generation following him was expanded by Euclid. Actually, Aristotle's work in mathematics was not one of his great contributions. To him, mathematics was primarily of value because it trained the mind for philosophy and because it supplied the reason for the facts which could be observed in astronomy, optics, and the study of music or harmony.

Nevertheless, mathematics, too, he was careful to point out, studied those ideas which could be separated from material objects—objects which, in fact, had to be dealt with in the abstract if they were to be properly understood. Among these were the ideas of straight and curved, odd and even, number, line and height.

True, all these branches of science have been enlarged upon by later scientists and, in some subjects such as astronomy, Aristotle's teaching is no longer completely valid; however, he did make an important contribution in two ways. First, he established the program of research which was followed in all later studies of mathematics and physics. Secondly, he provided a set of technical terms for use in physics. In some cases he had to invent the words, in other cases he gave an existing word a special meaning which it never lost. This meant that he saw the need for, and indeed provided, a terminology which would enable the human mind to understand the world of nature.

Aristotle's basic conviction was that it was possible to achieve knowledge. This conviction remained valid even in instances in which it was not possible for Aristotle himself to gain the final results, as for example, in chemistry, where later scientists were able to reach Aristotle's goals using equipment and research methods developed centuries after Aristotle.

This period in Athens is thought to be the time when Aristotle began setting down in book form the many notes he must have kept all during this lifetime of research. In addition to the notes, which were mentioned earlier as having been carefully preserved, there are the books which he wrote. These books are well-organized, planned treatises, and it is unlikely that they were put together during his years of "wandering" from Athens, to Assos, Mytilene, Pella, Stagira, and finally back to Athens.

The books that have been handed down through the ages contain almost all of Aristotle's discoveries, thoughts, and such opinions as he expressed—with the exception of his botanical researches. It is also believed that Aristotle probably did write a book about his discoveries in the field of botany but, if he did, it has been lost.

Also lost, apparently, are many of the notes in which Aristotle must have described the means he used to learn about the habits and life cycles of animals and fish. How, for example, did he manage to get close enough to a mother octopus to write such an accurate account of the way in which she gave birth to her young? How did he manage to keep track of one dolphin long enough to learn that it would be fully grown in ten years? It would be interesting to know the answers to these and many other questions, but the information, if it was ever written down, has been lost to us.

Indeed, we are fortunate to have any of Aristotle's writings at all. It seems that, after his death, Aristotle's writings were passed on to Neleus, the son of that same Coriscus with whom he had studied in Assos. Neleus took the writings to his family home in Scepsis, and there they remained, forgotten, stacked away in the cellar, for almost two hundred and fifty years. Not until the Roman Empire, under Sulla, were they discovered and brought back to the learned world. Fortunately, when the manuscripts were found, they could still be read.

These years in Athens were fruitful and contented ones for Aristotle. He had his school—and his friends—about him, and he had the time to continue his research and to write his treatises. Athens was then under the rule of Macedonia, Alexander by this time having conquered most of the known world. Aristotle was, of course, on the best of terms with the Madedonian rulers, because of his association with Alexander.

But there were others in Athens who were not at all happy with the situation. Many Greeks, inside and outside of the city, hated the idea of being under a foreign rule, even though Antipater—Alexander's regent in Greece— seems to have been a fair-minded governor. One of these Athenian dissenters was Demosthenes.

It is interesting to note that Demosthenes and Aristotle were born in the same year (384 B.C.) and died in the same year (322 B.C.). However, they followed very different careers. A native of Athens, Demosthenes was, from first to last, a patriotic citizen and a great Athenian statesman. Like Aristotle, Demosthenes became an orphan early in life, but unlike the fortunate Aristotle—whose guardian took good care of him—Demosthenes was placed in the hands of two of his father's nephews who proved to be unscrupulous men; they embezzled most of the money that Demosthenes should have inherited from his father.

The treachery of his guardians may have been the impetus that started Demosthenes on his career of public life. In order to get back his inheritance, he took up the study of law so that he could bring suit against his father's nephews. This was not easy for Demosthenes, because, to argue a case in court one had to be able to speak well, and Demosthenes had a very bad speech impediment (possibly he stuttered). By reciting poetry with his mouth full of pebbles, however, he was able to cure himself of the impediment. Demosthenes not only went on to win his case, but he also became a great orator in Athenian politics.

Demosthenes was unalterably against Macedonian domination of Greece. All during Philip's reign, Demosthenes had opposed him and had told the Greeks that they would be making a serious mistake to align themselves with Macedonia. There were a number of pro-Macedonian political parties within Athens seeking to persuade the Greeks that alignment with Philip would be good for Greece and, especially, for Athens. Demosthenes was, of course, thoroughly disliked by these supporters of Macedonia. When Philip died, Demosthenes celebrated, as though it were a great holiday.

Alexander was, of course, very displeased with this man who had so joyfully celebrated his father's death. He demanded that Demosthenes be handed over to him for punishment. The Athenians refused, and Alexander, wishing to remain on good terms with Athens, dropped the demand. So Demosthenes remained in Athens, continuing to speak against the Macedonian "tyrants," and continuing to encourage anti-Macedonian sentiments among the people of Athens.

It is doubtful whether Aristotle and Demosthenes ever had any contact with each other, since they were on opposite sides of the political "fence." Aristotle, content with his working, writing, and teaching, may not even have been aware of how much anti-Macedonian feeling there was in Athens.

Aristotle had spent eleven years in Athens, when suddenly his peace and quiet came to an end. News arrived in

Athens that Alexander, now thirty-two and in the process of conquering Babylonia, had died of a fever.

This news was greeted with joy by Demosthenes and the members of the nationalist movement in Athens. Antipater, Alexander's regent, was away from the city at the time; and, to the Athenians, it seemed that now was their chance to throw off the Macedonian rule for good.

Thus, the situation became very uneasy for Aristotle, who was a non-Athenian and well known for his connections with the Macedonian dynasty. It was not long before the anti-Macedonian parties began looking for ways to destroy him or, at least, drive him out of Athens.

They also remembered the ode that Aristotle had composed on the death of Hermias. This ode, though addressed to a human being, was written in the classic style of odes addressed to the gods. In addition, in the ode Aristotle had compared Hermias' courage in the face of Persian torture with the bravery of Achilles, one of the greatest heroes of Greece. To the enemies of Aristotle this was sacrilege. They accused him of trying to set Hermias up as a god.

The crime of impiety was a serious offense. Most Greeks of that age, not having studied nature as thoroughly as Aristotle, still believed that the gods controlled their lives and destinies. Anyone who showed a lack of reverence for the gods might very well bring down their wrath upon the entire city.

Aristotle realized the coming danger to himself. Leaving the Lyceum in the charge of his faithful friend Theophrastus, he left the city for the last time. Now sixty-one years old, Aristotle headed for his mother's home in the city of Chalcis on the island of Euboa, an area under Macedonian control. He did not have much longer to live, however. The following year he died, apparently of natural causes, and was buried in or near Chalcis.

Aristotle's school in Athens was continued by his old friend Theophrastus. Theophrastus as an alien was, as Aristotle had been, prohibited from purchasing property in Athens, but his pupil, the wealthy and powerful Demetrius of Phalerum, enabled him to purchase an estate for the school. Theophrastus, because of his connection with Aristotle, was subject to political attacks from the anti-Macedonian party in Athens, but he was able to maintain the school, and it continued to flourish under his successors.

Before he died, Aristotle had made a will, in order to provide for his family. This document is of interest to us because it shows that, in spite of his great devotion to research, study, and teaching, he was also a thoughtful husband and father. Not only did he make very careful provisions for his widow, Herpyllis (his first wife, Pythias, had died some years before), and his children, Pythias and Nicomachus; he also instructed that certain of his slaves should be freed while certain others, who were still very young, should be taken care of until they were old enough to look out for themselves and then set free.

At the end of this will, Aristotle thought back to his first wife, whom he had loved so much, and wrote: "And wherever they bury me, there the bones of Pythias shall be laid, in accordance with her own instructions."

EIGHTEEN

"The Master of Those Who Know"

When the Italian poet Dante Alighieri (1265–1321) wrote his *Divine Comedy* as an allegorical picture of the life after death, he placed Aristotle among the famous dead, honoring him with the title "The Master of Those Who Know." This phrase is a typical reflection of the veneration in which Aristotle was held during the Middle Ages. He was looked upon as the greatest philosopher and scientist that had ever lived. Indeed, his word amounted to law among all students.

In the eastern Mediterranean, the scholars of the Byzantine Empire in the Middle Ages still read and taught Aristotle's works in Greek. His writings were also translated into Arabic by order of the caliphs of the Moslem world, who were eager to make the treasures of Greek science and philosophy available to their people.

In western Europe, however, as the Roman Empire declined, the knowledge of Greek eventually died out and for a long time Aristotle was known only in the Latin translations of some of his works which had been made earlier. This was all that was known of Aristotle in the West. However, when the Arabs occupied the Spanish peninsula in their ever-widening conquests, they brought their own

translations of Aristotle with them. In time, European
scholars came into contact with their Moslem colleagues
in Spain and discovered the Arabic versions of Aristotle.
The discovery of Aristotle's writings preserved in Arabic
was an event of such importance that it was not long before
they were translated from Arabic into Latin, which was
then the universal scholarly tongue spoken and written
throughout Europe.

Thus, for a long time, Aristotle was known in Europe
only through a translation-of-a-translation. Yet this was,
in fact, the end of a long journey for the master's writings.
Aristotle's works had traveled from Athens to medieval
Constantinople, from thence to Moslem Bagdad, and there
were rendered into Arabic. From Bagdad and Syria the
books then traveled to North Africa; and from North
Africa to Spain. From Spain, in their new Latin dress, they
made their way to the great medieval universities of Italy,
France and England. Even in a translation-of-a-translation,
Aristotle was still regarded as the prince of philosophers
and scientists.

In time, however, Western scholars had the opportunity
to learn Greek from Byzantine travelers in Europe, who
gave lessons in their native tongue. Then, with the capture
of Constantinople by the Turks in 1453, many Greek scholars were driven to the west, carrying their precious manuscripts with them. So it was that Aristotle came in original
Greek text to the European scholars of the Renaissance
when they were beginning to revive the literary treasures
of antiquity. Once more Aristotle could be read in the
original.

Moreover, the invention about this same time of printing
from movable type meant that copies of Aristotle's works,

either in the original Greek or in Latin translation, could be widely circulated. More translations were made of the works of Aristotle during the 1400's than of any other ancient Greek author. In Italy before 1450, over forty of Aristotle's manuscripts can be traced, including copies of all of his important works, whereas at the same time there were only twenty manuscripts of the works of Plato, and still fewer of other classical authors.

In the Middle Ages, thinkers had accepted all of Aristotle's conclusions without question. His prestige was enormous. He was, in fact, the only writer who offered a complete system of knowledge, and he was the only philosopher who appeared to provide answers for what seemed to be every question that could be asked. Indeed, a new idea could not gain approval unless it agreed with the teaching of Aristotle.

With the arrival of the Renaissance, however, the whole world of learning and science began to change. Scientists found themselves not only in the midst of the physical expansion of the world in which they lived, but also in the expansion of their intellectual world. They began to realize that they were independent of the limitations of tradition. They began new experimental work, and improvements in the making of machinery and apparatus meant that new fields of research were opened up. The man of the Renaissance, finding new avenues of thought widening out on all sides around him, felt free to follow his own interests and determine his own results.

Yet, for Aristotle, the coming of the Renaissance spelled defeat for certain portions of his carefully built-up system of knowledge. Astronomy in particular had made great advances among the Arabs during the Middle Ages, as well as in the Christian world, and it was becoming plain that here Aristotle's system could no longer be upheld. The Polish astronomer, Nicolaus Copernicus (1473–1543), demonstrated that the earth rotated on its axis and revolved about the sun, and that the planets revolved in orbits around the sun. Later, the great German astronomer, Johannes Kepler, described the motion of the planets more correctly.

Thus there began a battle in which, for a time, Aristotle lost ground. The champions of the new revival of learning attacked the supporters of Aristotle as being ultraconservative and even reactionary. But the Aristotelians remained in power in many places and they succeeded in blocking the astronomical work of Italian scientists like Giordano Bruno and Galileo. They were even strong enough to drive Bruno out of the University of Paris in 1583, and Galileo out of Pisa, the great university center, in 1591.

Actually, of course, most of the thinking of the Renaissance scholars went on *within* the framework of ideas and methods established by Aristotle. In fact, the "modern scientists" of that day had to use his terms even if they rebelled against his teaching. If, during this period, Aristotle as a scientist seemed to be "overthrown," it was partly because contemporary scientists, themselves trained on Aristotle's works, were using his writings as a springboard for their own new discoveries.

Yet new advances were bound to come. The invention of the microscope and the telescope opened up a whole new era in biology and astronomy. When Galileo's telescopes became available, the sky was filled with new things, and the improved microscopes of Anton Leeuwenhoek (1632–1723) made it possible to observe very tiny organisms for the first time. In Aristotle's day, of course, these were not available. Still, it is important to remember how much Aristotle was able to accomplish without them.

Although Aristotle's physics was shown to be inadequate, and his astronomy was overthrown, he regained his position of enormous prestige with the development of the modern biological sciences in the 18th and 19th centuries. Scientists began to rediscover Aristotle's work. Indeed, their confirmation of his results and observations bore testimony to the painstaking excellence of his scientific spirit. Today, even though Aristotle is no longer in direct competition with modern science, he can be appreciated for what his great and inquiring mind did for the minds of other men.

If, by some supernatural means, Aristotle could visit the modern world and see how much of his work has been replaced, would he be disappointed? It is most probable that he would not; for any scientist hopes and strives for progress. Rather, it would doubtless please Aristotle to know that his work had laid the groundwork for something better. For Aristotle was always well aware that he himself had had to start out on the basis of what his predecessors had done.

It is also fairly certain that Aristotle would not be displeased to discover that some people were using his methods and technical terms without realizing that he, Aristotle, had invented them. On the contrary, it would surely give him great satisfaction to know that his achievements had become so much a basic part of science today.

Aristotle's life shows what a man of genius is capable of leaving behind him. His legacy consists of two parts. First, of course, are his actual scientific and philosophic accomplishments. Some of these may prove to be permanent; others may in time be replaced.

But the second part of Aristotle's legacy might well be

ranked as even more important—namely, the example and permanent influence of a man of true genius. In other words, it is Aristotle's gift to civilization that he left the world a different place to live in after his own death. He gave something of his mind and spirit to all men—whether or not they realize it.

Thus, Aristotle's name still lives on today. True, his works concerning biology and logic remain best known to moderns. Yet Aristotle's ultimate goal reached far beyond those studies. Indeed, that ultimate goal—of which this famous Greek was always conscious—was the complete study of man.

Moreover, by reason and argument, he sought to prove the existence of a God who was good. To Aristotle, God was an ever-living Being, good in His essential nature, and thus good for man.

Aristotle's biological work in particular convinced him that if one studies everything that exists, it will be certain that it exists for a purpose. God is at work in the world, Aristotle believed, and, as he wrote, "God and nature do nothing in vain."

So it can be seen that while Aristotle was occupied with the study of nature he thought of his studies as leading to a knowledge of God.

By trying to understand Aristotle's mind and his work, we can better understand what our own generation is and how it came into being. We can, in a way, make our understanding of life more meaningful by going back to the roots of the human spirit as they developed in Aristotle and other such men. Thus we ourselves find confidence in the future yet to be built.

Index